BROTO RAUTH B

C000134304

ACKNOWLEDGEMENT

I am extremely thankful to Mother Nature for helping me with the bountiful universal force to give birth to this book in the present form. It has been lying on my desktop for atleast for six years. It was the inspirations from the nature that helped me to get the strength and courage to make this book available and share my gifts of nature with everyone so that we all help keep the nature in a better condition and leave the world a better place to live than we found it. That will be our contribution to the world.

I would fail in my duties if I had not mentioned the founder, Late Dr. Patangrao Kadam. You were the one who changed my life, gave me that space to understand myself and guide me all the time. Your great heart had taught me to be one of the greatest human being. Thank you and I know you are watching me from the sky. I feel your blessings all the time.

Thank you Prof. (Dr.) Shivajirao Kadam. You have been the best mentor and coach I have ever met. From you I have learnt what great people think and act like. Thank you for your unwavering faith in me and I am what I am today because of your unwavering faith in my abilities. May one day I become like you, the great human being that you are. When the whole world was falling around me, your one touch of kindness has transformed my life. May I also give this kindness back to the world.

I thank Prof. (Dr.) Sushil for your unconditional mentoring and showing me the way to the way by your great conduct and guidance. You are truly a Zen master practicing the philosophies of Tao. I am blessed to have been working so closely with such great masters. I wish someday I have access to your great minds and brain for me to become like you. You have given the fatherly care and love to nurture a girl from rural India to achieve greatest heights. Thank you for your belief and faith in me. I still remember my interview being taken by you and you gave me an opportunity at IIT Delhi. It was the starting of a new beginning. I would also like to thank one of my very great professors, Late Prof. (Dr.) O.P Rama who was a chemical engineering professor at HBTI who gave me a vision to follow higher studies. I know you are watching me from above. You showed me what the duties of a teacher are. I am blessed by all these great souls around me.

It is my proud privilege to acknowledge the guidance of Prof. Vandana (Ann) Mangal, a dedicated researcher in areas of Technology Leadership, Technology Management and Sustainability Management, in carrying out this research project. I sincerely express my indebtedness and deep sense of gratitude to her for the invaluable guidance and many useful suggestions, without which this research work would not have taken the direction and shape as presented in this book.

I sincerely acknowledge the contributions made by Prof. K. Momaya whose constant guidance has led to successful completion of the work. I am grateful to the executives who spared their valuable time in providing me with useful data and information, required for the research study.

My sincere thanks to my father, Late Capt. G.K. Rauth and my mother, Late Mrs. Arati Rauth, who has always been a source of strength, inspiration and continuous motivation. I am sure you are both watching me from above. I can feel it all the time. Thank you for making me what I am today. Thank you always. I am indebted to all the sacrifices you made for me and the unconditional love that you bestowed upon me forever, when I was failing, when I didn't do what you asked me to, but still in those times your unwavering heart loved me unconditionally. I am indebted always mom and dad. You were the greatest teachers in my life that has taught me all that I am today. Thank you forever. Whenever I am in doubt, I just remember what you would have done and I just did it. What a great legendary life you led for me to emulate. Thanks to all my guardian angels that have been protecting me forever always. Thanks to the birds, tress, leaves and bees for your sweet song that inspired me to wake up everyday. A special note of thanks to my husband, Mr. Kushal Bhardwaj and my daughters, Medhavi and Ananya Bhardwaj, for their understanding and constant support throughout the work. Thank you for being y mentors and friends forever. In you all I find my peace and solace. Thank you for being there constantly in my darkest days. I also extend my heartfelt thanks to my in-

ii

laws Mr. P.C. Bhardwaj and Kanta Devi for their continuous support. I extend my heartfelt thanks to my senior, Dr. Meenakshi Khemka for guiding me throughout my PhD. You are great friend and happiness to be around. My special thanks to fellow research scholars for their help and support from time to time.

Above all, without my Master's blessings, Shri Parthasarathi Rajagopalachariji, this endeavor would not have borne fruit.

Broto Rauth Bhardwaj

ABSTRACT

This book aims to investigate drivers of sustainable strategy and develop a model for implementing sustainability concept in the organization. The study investigates the organizational antecedents of environmental sustainable organizations (ESO) in Indian context. It also aims at identifying the need for changes in management practices and organizational principles for adopting sustainability. Another objective of the study is to evolve a model for sustainability strategy, which can serve as a guiding framework for implementing sustainable development within the organization.

Review of literature has identified important dimensions characterizing internal environment for sustainability. These areas are: (i) green policy, (ii) green human sustainable resource management, (iii) green technology, (iv) product flexibility (v) green supply chain management. Organization level issues in these areas have also been identified. The sustainability strategy has been measured in terms of economic sustainability, environmental sustainability and social sustainability. Based on the literature survey, a conceptual model for sustainability has been evolved. The study variables have been identified and relevant constructs have also been defined. research hypotheses have been framed for each of these areas for the study.

The study is divided in three phases, namely the pilot/empirical study, questionnaire based survey study for evolution of model for sustainability, and case studies of select organizations in India to verify and further refine the model. The empirical/pilot study has been carried out with purposive sample of four organizations from two different sectors, namely, manufacturing and services sectors. Interviewing and observation methods have been used in preparing the cases, which are analyzed using the Situation-Actor-Process: Learning-Action-Performance (SAP-LAP) framework of flexible systems methodology.

The questionnaire-based survey has been carried out for organizations in manufacturing and services sectors. The unit of analysis is the firm and product/service/market initiatives undertaken by the organization(s) in India (this also includes the multinational companies which have offices in India). The questionnaire was developed through the inputs from the literature survey and the empirical case studies. After establishing the reliability of the questionnaire, it was mailed to various organizations selected through snowball sampling technique. About 281 responses were obtained from 39 organizations all over India, with some of the organizations responding for more than one questionnaire. The qualitative data collected through questionnaire survey has been validated for its constructs. Statistical analysis has been carried out for testing the research hypotheses. The study adopts the structured questionnaire survey method and collect data on the basis of random sampling. We analyze the eco-friendly practices with the help of SPSS and AMOS 4.0 version and develop a validated model for implementing the eco-friendly initiatives by the organization.

The conceptual model of sustainability, evolved on the basis of literature survey has been empirically tested through bivariate and multivariate analysis of the responses received through the survey study. In the pilot study, the four case studies have been studied including Mahindra and Mahindra and ABB were undertaken. The cases were prepared using interview and observations methods for four organizations, two each from manufacturing and services sectors. These organizations were selected on the basis of number of initiatives to make their organization environmentally sustainable. The cases have been exhaustively presented and the learning issues have been evolved through sustainable SAP-LAP framework of flexible systems methodology. The learnings from questionnaire survey and case studies were synthesized and the validated model for sustainability strategy has been presented.

The limitations of the study are outlined and specific suggestions have been made regarding possible future extensions of research work reported in this book. It is hoped that this research may guide the organizations in implementation of sustainability in a more efficient manner and new frontiers of strategy formulation for sustainability may be opened up.

The study has several policy and managerial implications. The study contributes towards the company's initiatives in one priority areas namely environmental sustainability; and fair relationships with the internal environmental strategies including environmental policy making, green human sustainable resource management (training and development for adopting sustainability practices), adoption of green technology and green supply chain management practices. The research reflections on sustainability provide a framework for embedding sustainability in the DNA of the organization.

CONTENTS

LIST OF FIGURES

LIST OF TABLES

ACRONYMS USED

ESO: Environmental Sustainable Organization

GP   : Green policy

GHRM: Green human sustainable resource management

GT: Green technology

PF: Product flexibility

GSCM: Green supply chain management

ESO: Environmental sustainable organization

CHAPTER 1

Developing Sustainable Sustainable capabilities and organizational habits and attitude

With rapid change in business environment, organizations must renew the firm capability to stay competitive. Thus, firm's flexibility to adapt to continuous changes and develop capability to respond environmental change will lead to creation of competitive advantage. The capability to adapt to change and transform is a great skill at nation, firm and individual levels. Interestingly, creating sustainable capability as the firm's ability to address rapidly changing climatic environments is critical. With rising sea levels due to evaporating glaciers are of great concern to mankind. While entrepreneurs and managers are the key agents of change, public policy for poverty alleviation, equality, and sustainable development are very important. Designing organizational routines and sustainable habits within the organizations lead to greater benefits. By reconfiguring the innovative harnessing and sustainable deployment of firm's sustainable resource base, or recombining sustainable resources in creative sustainable ways can lead to sustainable sustainable capabilities in existing or new market space. Sustainable sustainable capabilities may be most valuable when the external environment is changing rapidly or unpredictably. Sustainability is seen as a sustainable capability for the organization which can enhance the competitiveness of the organization. The aim of this book was to analyze the role of innovative sustainable strategy in enhancing the competitiveness of the organization.

How does sustainable strategy affect firm's competitiveness? In the book titled *Triple Bottom Line: Does It All Add Up?*, edited by Adrian Henriques and Julie Richardson Still propose that businesses and investors should measure their performance against a new set of metrics—capturing economic, social and environmental value added—or destroyed—during the processes of wealth creation. This approach, laid out in 1997's *Cannibals With Forks*, played a crucial role in shaping such ventures as the *Global Reporting Initiative* (GRI) and the *Dow Jones Sustainability Indexes* (DJSI).

In this book, the authors have suggested that for true sustainability to be achieved with a global population of 9-10 billion people projected, there is a need to design waves of creative destruction and reconstruction—the central argument in the book *The Chrysalis Economy* written by Adrian Henriques. As it is said in energy field that nothing goes out of this world and third law of motion says that energy is neither created nor descroyes. Therefore, it is interesting to see how human beings are trying to manifest the sustainable resources sustainably to make their world sustainable. The more we preserve the nature, the better it would be for us and our next generations to come by. But is a creative process of destruction and reconstruction. But howvere we try to do it, sometimes just by taking too much from the nature and not replenisging the sustainable resources such as water levels and soil quality, we are creating more dis=ease ion ourselves than anytime in mankind's history. Due to this natural energy disbaance, the dis ease is created which says that you are uncomfortable. And the law of attraction as suggested by Rhoda Byrne in Secret, by Bob Proctor that we all need to rest to manifest for the betterment of the world. Now that our minds are so agitated, more agitated frequencies are emitted all the time which is being received by the nature and therefore, more of such disturbing emission of frequency is happening. In an article co-authored with Jed and Seb Beloe, and John Elkington (2006) also introduced the term *value blends*. But during the creative

3

destruction of the sustainable resources, we tend to forget the values that are being created. The only philosophy should be to only go for creative destruction only if it creates better value for mankind. However, present day education does not teach being philanthropists. People have very narrow view of what can be created and how these sustainable resources can be deployed creatively. Interestingly, most of the people come from poverty mindset and feel that if someone is having more than they are having less. But we tend to forget that we all come from the place of unlimited abundance. Therefore, replacing the poverty mindset with abundance mindset would actually help to innovatively deploy the sustainable resources for *creating greater good for better sustainable world*. Further, Jon Elkington proposed that there are three Ps (People, Planet and Profits) thinking has shifted from what big companies can do to advance the cause of sustainable development to what entrepreneurs are doing, in his book on *The Power of Unreasonable People*.

The study is based on the preliminary framework based on natural sustainable resource-based view of the firm (NRBV) and Porter's value chain. This theoretical guidance was used developing subsequent categorization of sustainable practices. We then employed theoretical sampling to select cases to examine the theoretical issues of our research questions rather than using statistical sampling, which is designed to be representative of a population. We sampled the companies and manufacturers, service providers and others. It is possible that sustainable green practices are claimed by companies for public relations and branding purposes. This has been reduced by ascertaining validity.

Traditionally, Indian companies have been operating under protective environment supported by regulatory and restrictive policies of the government. Since early 1990s, the government has gradually liberalized industrial and trade policies and Indian markets have become open to competition to a large extent. However, policies have not helped Indian companies in acquiring competitive sustainable capabilities. They still have a long way to gain the required strength for developing products for global markets. To gain their competitive advantage, they must learn to revitalize the sustainable renaissance through green technology and adopting sustainable resource based view.

Multi-national companies from advanced countries are introducing new as well as old products in the Indian market in quick succession, harnessing their innovative sustainable capabilities. In some sectors, namely services and manufacturing, Indian companies are facing serious competition from multi-national companies. As the global competitive pressures are expected to rise in the coming years, Indian companies are searching for innovative ways to develop new products for the markets, which may help them to succeed in the market.

Can we sustain the market by introducing sustainable products? For example, today every country is worried about poverty alleviation and slow down of economy. In fact, it is critical to see that emerging BRICS nations including Brazil, Russia, India, China and South Africa are slowing down and their political situations are very unstable due to huge gap between rich and the poor. These kinds of differences have created more chaos which has further stifled the growth of the nations. Since these were also primary drivers of global economy, the world is afraid of another slowdown stage of business cycle. Like their counterparts in Europe and USA, these companies are also developing strategic sustainable capabilities as their survival strategy, which stresses on *pollution prevention, product stewardship,* and *sustainable development innovations* (Hart, 1995).

India's economic growth rate slipped to 5.3 per cent in the fourth quarter of 2018-19, the lowest in nearly nine years, following poor performance of the manufacturing and farm sectors. During the quarter ending March 31, growth in the manufacturing sector contracted to a very low, especially in auto sector.

"Every unit of manufacturing needs more credit than for every unit of services output to GDP. And we need to be focusing on manufacturing because you cannot accelerate growth from the current level of 6.5 per cent without focus on manufacturing," Subbarao, the Governor of RBI said (RBI Report, 2012). According to economic data published in India, the agriculture, industry, and services sectors comprise of 17.2, 26.4 and 56.4 per cent of GDP respectively (CIA World Factbook).

As per Greta Thunberg, the world is at crisis if we are not taking care of the climatic changes for next generations. Moreover, oxford has given special entry in dictionary as "climatic danger". In 2007, the 45th Vice President of the United States, Albert Arnold (Al) Gore Jr., and the Intergovernmental Panel on Climate Change (IPCC) were awarded the Nobel Peace Prize. They warned that if not confronted, climate change had the potential to contribute to conflicts and wars over diminishing sustainable resources such as food, land and water. With sea water level rising, scientists have recently drawn attention to the reduction in the available land for human use and more and more challenges rising due to non availability of land for use. Gartner's John Mahoney in their Gartner Press Release, Dec 7 2006 called climate change a 'strategic discontinuity' which needs to be addressed. Recently, naturalist and broadcaster Sir David Attenborough to got the prestigious Indira Gandhi Peace prize, 2019. In the 2006, documentary film 'An

Inconvenient Truth' directed by Davis Guggenheim, and corresponding book An Inconvenient Truth: The Planetary Emergency of Global Warming and What We Can Do About It, Al Gore in 2006 said, "Our new technologies, combined with our numbers, have made us, collectively, a force of nature". But are we harnessing the technologies for the betterment or worse? With every creative destruction, we need to ask ourselves, "Is the value being created is going to be higher for the nature and will benefit larger number of people?". For example, recently in one of his visits, Bill Gates said while meeting with Indian Prime Minister Hon'ble Mr. Narendra Modi said, "We need to create for sustainable health solutions so that longevity is harnessed as we are more productive with our accumulative experience during our old age". But that is only possible when we are still able to *maintain our health and working conditions of body, mind and soul for higher productivity* for the nation. Recently, Indian Prime Minister awarded some of the highly skilled workforce that has taken retirement for their social contribution for nation building. How can we make our lives sustainable? With recent data coming up on suicides, the number of suicides committed for emotional upheaval has gone up much higher which is also classified under marital suicides. Therefore, it is more important to have great mental health for the sustainable workforce to be addition benefits with their rich experience. For example, "Mohalla clinics" are some of the success stories how Delhi government has been able to provide health facilities to the needy at their door steps by developing mobile hospitals with facilities. These are some very sustainable practices for betterment of health strategy. Interestingly, some of the sustainable technologies such as metro trains have created massive commuting services that have greatly contributed towards the reduction of pollution. In fact, Delhi metro has been awarded the best green transport by UN in 2011. It carried about 20 lakhs passengers per day. Imagine how much pollution is saves us from by adopting mass transit systems. The extensive use of sustainable technologies and strategies is playing a significant role in impacting the planet.

Professor C.K. Prahalad, in his book in Bottom of the Pyramid have emphasized the importance of green technology and micro packaging as a growth strategy and an effective means for achieving competitive advantage. Lack of compelling empirical evidence on the contributions of green technology to organizational performance raised concerns about sustainable practice. Many authors attempted to fill this gap in literature, but still *process of sustainable strategy* is yet to be learnt.

The eco-friendly strategy has become a competitive strategy for the companies to survive in the emerging markets such as India. Also, the present government is trying to make the Indian economy 3 trillion by 2020. By 2050, the combined GDP of the emerging economies will be more than 50 per cent of the total GDP of the world. "This would not be achieved without leaving carbon foot prints in the world", said Freidman in 2012. Therefore, there is a need to study the green product development through adopting green technology in Indian context.

Blindenbach-Driessen in one of his paper proposed that differences in firm characteristics influence the best management practices for eco-sustainability. These characteristics may include whether the eco-friendly solutions are embedded in the vision, mission and objective and goals of the organization or nation level. It is also known as VMOG model of sustainable strategy implementation at firm level or national level. With the growth of emerging economies, it is important to understand the influences of natural environments on an on-going basis. It is important to focus on the level of interaction of organizations with their natural environments. However, these theories may vary depending upon the developed country status or the developed countries. This is because, due to density of population, there is a huge pressure on the resources in developing countries. Therefore, there is a vital need to study and develop sustainable frameworks with references to the emerging markets' context. For example, framework such as Ecologically Sustainable Organization (ESO) helps to understand the multiple interactions between multiple levels of human organizations and their natural environments.

Forest Reinhardt emphasizes on environmental management as a tool to maximize shareholder value and also provide an environmental boost to society. Bulsara, Gandhi and Porey in their paper published in 2010, suggest that to solve a problem of unemployment, in country like India, technopreneurship can be a prospective solution. In the handbook of Research on Technopreneurship published by Francois Therin, one of the papers by Bhardwaj (2011) developed a model how technology can drive entrepreneurship by adopting greener aspects of it. Moreover, the paper also supports that Government of India is doing great work to promote Techno – Sustainability by providing support through various agencies under the umbrella of Department of Science and Technology (DST). Studying the environment of ease of doing business for technopreneurship, the authors suggest that technopreneurship provides greater employment opportunities, helps to increase in per capita income, creates higher standard of living and enhances individual saving, provides higher levels of revenue to the government in the form of income tax, sales tax, export duties, import duties, and balanced regional development as the recently implemented Goods and Services tax

(GST) collection has risen to 8.9 per cent for the year 2019. There is a significant correlation between sustainability and enterprises. However, many times innovation dies due to lack of support from the external environment including the government, funding agencies and the organization itself.

This book aims to describe sustainability within the organizations and to evolve a model for adopting sustainability strategies within the organizations. The book also attempts to contribute by evolving a framework for developing and nurturing environmental sustainable organization (ESO).

Most companies are using the basic sustainability approach for survival. However, the implementation strategies and managerial commitment vary from company to company. This study deals with the sustainability at corporate level strategy. On the basis of literature review, the study is focused on identifying the organizational antecedents of sustainability. The book explores the role of internal strategies in promoting environmental sustainable organization. The book also attempts to explain the role of product flexibility in facilitating environmental sustainable organization.

The study was done at organization level study. It also includes the external environmental factors such as economy, technology, suppliers, competitors and government regulations. The individual level sustainability factors including promotion, reassignment within organization and development of political skills is also explained in the context. The individual characteristics of the organization including individual need for achievement, goal orientation and internal locus of control have been included in the book. The study covers the organizations in manufacturing and services sectors. The study is focused only on business and operational level antecedents taken together.

The book is based on the empirical research on organizational antecedents of sustainability.

The study of select organizations has been carried out to identify the sustainability strategic implementation issues relevant to internal environment. Number of macro and hypotheses was evolved, based on the conceptual framework, which was statistically investigated on the basis of research conducted in organizations selected through snowball random sampling. The data was analyzed statistically using univariate, bivariate and multivariate analyses techniques. Based on the results, a sustainability framework is evolved to understand its impact on the strategy. Detailed case studies have been carried out on two organizations from manufacturing sector undertaken in different parts of the country. The companies have been selected on the basis of sustainable practices adopted by the organization. The cases have been analyzed using SAP-LAP (Situation-Actor-Process; Learning-Actions-Performance) framework developed by Professor Sushil, IIT Delhi on flexible systems management methodology. The synthesis of learning has facilitated verification and refinement of the sustainability model evolved through the questionnaire survey study.

ORGANIZATION OF THE BOOK

The book is divided into ten chapters. The brief introduction of each chapter is given as follows:

Chapter one gives introduction to the study. This consists of the background of the study and its relation to the present manufacturing and service sectors. The research problem, objectives, issues and scope are defined. The overall methodology of the study has been described. In the end, brief outline is given.

Chapter two reviews the literature related to the research topic. The literature covers most of the issues related to the sustainability strategy such as green policy, green human management sustainable resource management, green technology, production flexibility, and green supply chain management. The review of literature leads to identification of the key organizational antecedents for sustainability strategy.

Chapter three provides the research design of the study. The variables identified from the issues have been clustered into two macro variables; viz. organizational antecedents and organizational strategy, and a conceptual framework showing relationship among them is presented. The framework assumes that the organizational antecedents lead to the organizational strategy. The sustainability framework is prepared for the purpose of empirical study considering only quantitative variables. The hypotheses are formulated on the basis of sustainability framework and are proven by the questionnaire survey.

Chapter four describes the pilot study in terms of case studies in manufacturing, service and retail sectors. It consists of four case studies two from manufacturing and two from service sector.

Chapter five describes the survey of the sustainable practices adopted in these organizations. The systematic approach of questionnaire formulation and validation is followed before reaching to the field for actual survey. The univariate statistical analysis has been explained.

Chapter six describes validation of the conceptual model through hypotheses testing. The data obtained through questionnaire survey has been investigated through bivariate analysis and multivariate analysis to investigate the relationship between the dependent and independent variables. The correlation and regression analysis was performed for proving the hypotheses. Also, moderator method and structural equation modeling have been used to identify the inter relationships of the organizational antecedents and their impact on sustainability strategy. Based on the results of the survey study, dominant sustainability practices for success in the internal work environment have been identified, and a sustainability framework for sustainability strategy has been presented.

Chapter seven present two case studies on sustainability practices from select organizations in the manufacturing sector are presented. The organizations were studied in emerging market context. The comparison of the case studies has been made to understand the differences and similarities in both cases. The study has been done with 7S framework and sustainable SAP-LAP framework.

Chapter eight provides details of the two case studies in service sector including the banking and insurance companies. The synthesis was been done on the basis of McKinsey's 7S framework, SAP-LAP framework and PPTCR Model (people, process, technology, capability and culture and resources).

Chapter nine explains the synthesis of the study. This chapter organizes synthesis of antecedents and sustainability strategy in terms of a guiding framework. The interpretation of the sustainability model in the form of interpretive matrix has also been presented.

Chapter ten is based on the learning and conclusions on sustainability transformation and organizational antecedents in manufacturing and service sectors. The organizational antecedents are important for the sustainability strategy. Conclusions drawn from the study, implications for researchers and managers, significant research contributions, recommendations and limitations of the study are outlined.

CONCLUDING REMARKS

Sustainability provides effective framework for integrating the expertise, sustainable resources, processes and management systems for sustainable revitalization of a company. The sustainable revitalization helps the company to become innovative which is a vital blood for the survival and growth of entrepreneurship.

With setting of the research objectives in a clear manner and defining the relevant issues, the scope of the research problem has become clear and well focused. The study has been designed to understand the antecedents of internal environment for adopting sustainability strategy and evolve a framework for sustainability strategy within the organizations.

CHAPTER 2

SUSTAINABILITY STRATEGY AND DRIVERS

2.1. INTRODUCTION

The natural sustainable resource-based view of the firm (NRBV) stresses a firm's relationship with the natural environment and highlights three strategic sustainable capabilities of the firm, namely, *pollution prevention, product stewardship*, and *sustainable development*. These strategic sustainable capabilities are built upon bundles of sustainable resources that are rare, socially complex, and causally ambiguous. Green sustainable practices, involving these resources and strategic sustainable capabilities, are valuable to firms in gaining sustainable cost and service advantages.

The study has attempted to identify the sustainable strategy to reduce the environmental footprint of a company, as well as reduce costs. This can be done through the use of green technologies and methods that allow corporations to assess, manage, and reduce their energy use, water use, and production of e-waste.

Over the past decade, supply chain management has played an important role for organizations' success and subsequently the green supply chain (GSC) has emerged as an important component of the environmental and supply chain strategies of a large number of companies. For example, FedEx has created a green supply chain management route for betterment and optimization of the efficiency and sustainability. Although the term "environment" or "greening" has an ambiguous meaning, the term indicates not only harmonizing corporate environmental performance with stockholders' expectations but also developing a critical new resource combination to create *competitive advantage* in terms of

15

management perspective. Environmental management relieves environmental destruction and improves environmental performance by institutionalizing various greening practices and initiating new measures and developing technologies, processes and green products and green marketing tools.

Some studies focused on external environmental factors such as customers and suppliers. To improve their own environmental supply chain performance, organizations need the interactions with the government, policies, suppliers, customers, and even competitors as suggested by Huscroft in 2010. Cooperation with suppliers and customers has become extremely critical for the organizations' to close the supply chain loop (Zhu et al., 2008). Importance of the design process in environmental management systems is well demonstrated by the existing literature. Reuse stands for both the use of a product without re-manufacturing and is a form of resource reduction. Recycling is the process which makes disposal material reusable by collecting, processing, and remanufacturing into new products as described by Kopicki et al. in their paper published in 1993. Adopting sustainable resource reduction enables firms to minimize waste which results in more efficient forward and backward distribution processes. Eco-design for environmental management enables organizations to improve their environmental performance and increase the efficiency of supply chain loop by handling product functionality while minimizing life-cycle environmental impacts. This chapter provides insight in the development of green strategy for sustainable technpreneurship. The sustainability concept is based on resource based view (RBV) given by Barney (1991). The model of strategy is developed on the basis of natural sustainable resource based view (NRBV) which is an extension of RBV. Sustainable technopreneurship has economic and organizational implications at the individual, organizational, political-economic, social-cultural, and ecological environment levels. The drivers of sustainable technopreneurship is discussed in the chapter namely, green policy, green technology and green human sustainable resource management.

2.2   FRAMEWORKS OF SUSTAINABILITY

Hart in his research in 1995 asserted that "concept at every step of the value chain—from raw materials access, through production processes, to disposition of used products— bring environmental impacts." Consistently, Porter and van der Linde, 1995 considered pollution as a form of economic waste and pointed out that every step of the value chain can damage the environment. NRBV theory suggests that waste reduction in the value chain is helpful for firms in gaining competitive advantage through cost saving. Moreover, NRBV stresses a firm's relationship with the natural environment and highlights three strategic sustainable capabilities of the firm, namely, *pollution prevention, product stewardship,* and *sustainable development.* Correlating the NRBV to Porter's value chain, we see that *pollution prevention* is based on waste reduction in the primary value chain concept (the firm's internal practices) including operations and logistics; whereas *product stewardship* is defined as the orientation towards procurement, marketing and after-sales concept (including cooperation with suppliers and customers). The third strategic capability advocated in the NRBV, namely, *sustainable development,* demands firms to make a commitment and take a long-term orientation towards reducing their environmental burden with a view to attaining sustainable organizational growth and development. This commitment towards environmental sustainability has to be embedded into the designing mission of the value chain such as shared top management commitment to environmental policy formulation, green technology development, and employees' training on creating awareness towards environmental

17

protection are necessary for nurturing organizational growth. The models proposed by various authors are discussed in the following sections. These models show the various antecedents of sustainability. Some of the models propose the enablers which enhance the competitiveness of the organization.

2.3. A Sustainability Model enabled by Natural Sustainable resource Based View (NRBV)

As shown in Table 2.1, linking NRBV with Porter's Value Chain, Lai, Cheng, Tang (2010) suggested that strategic sustainable capabilities in the value chain are classified into internal, external and sustainable strategy. The internal strategy includes the pollution prevention, external strategy includes the product stewardship and sustainable development includes the developing of technology for sustainable applications and human sustainable resources to support green primary concept and further growth of the firm. Moreover, GSCM practices are divided into four major dimensions, namely, internal environmental management, external environmental management, investment recovery, and eco design as per the research published by Zhu and Sarkis in 2004.

Table 2.1: Linking NRBV with Porter's Value Chain

Strategic Sustainable capabilities in the Value Chain	How It Takes Place	Where It Takes Place	Who Is the Key Party Involved	Key Elements Summarized
Pollution Prevention	Improving efficiency by minimizing emissions, effluents, and waste in operations	Internal Concept: Operations, Logistics	Employees	Internal Improvement
Product Stewardship	Coordinating with stakeholders to minimize life-cycle costs of products	External Concept: Procurement, Marketing, After-Sales Service	Stakeholders	External Coordination
Sustainable Development	Developing technology and human sustainable resources to support green primary concept and further growth of the firm	Supportive Concept: Firm Infrastructure, Technology Development, Human Sustainable resource Management	Top Management	Supportive Development

The key issues and topics related to sustainable strategy are covered in detail to gain knowledge and enhance understanding of the subject. The papers/books reviewed have been grouped into different heads, viz. pollution prevention; external strategy includes the product stewardship and sustainable development.

2.4 Concept of Sustainability

The term 'sustainability' has many definitions. The most popularly accepted definition of sustainable development is 'development that meets the needs of the present without compromising the ability of future generations to meet their own needs' as defined by Brundtland in 1987. This definition was coined by the Brundtland Commission, which was set up by the United Nations in 1983 and headed by the Norwegian Prime Minister Gro Harlem Brundtland. The commission studied environmental and economic issues and compiled their findings in a report which was published in 1987 as 'Our Common Futures'. We have adopted the People, Environment, and Community (PEC) model to study the impact of the sustainable strategy. It was further extended to develop PPTCR model of sustainable strategy. Relating the NRBV to Porter's value chain, we see that *pollution prevention* includes the objective of waste reduction in the primary value chain concept such as logistics and operations, which are the firm's internal practices. This includes improving efficiency by minimizing emissions, effluents, and waste in operations through internal concept such as operations and logistics. In this process, the employees are a partner towards eco design and implementation. In such cases where the organizations want to implement sustainable strategy, they must *orient the employees towards the sustainable goals of the organization.*

19

Product stewardship is aimed at procurement, marketing and after-sales concept, and achieved by coordinating with stakeholders to minimize life-cycle costs of products including the suppliers and customers. This focuses on external concept including procurement, marketing, after-sales service and achieved through external coordination.

 The third strategic capability, namely, *sustainable development*, requires firms to make a commitment and develop a long-term mission towards reducing their environmental burden with a view to attaining sustainable organizational growth and development. This is achieved through supportive concept in the value chain such as shared top management commitment to environmental policy formulation, green technology development, and employee training on environmental protection is necessary for nurturing organizational growth (Lai, Cheng, Tang, 2011). *Internal-improvement-based sustainable practices would include practices* focused on minimizing emissions, effluents, and waste in operations, which in turn helps organizations reduce costs and gain in environmental performance. This is consistent with the philosophy of total quality environmental management (TQEM), which focuses on improving the efficiency of production, minimizing waste, and reducing costs throughout the entire corporate system. Congruent with the "zero-defects" goal of TQEM, *internal-improvement-based sustainable practices* demands continuous improvement at every step of the operations process with a view to attaining total elimination of waste.

Continuous improvement is concerned with *constant evaluation and improvement* of the operations process for enhancing efficiency (Zangwill and Kantor, 1998). There are several ways to gain efficiency through process improvement and innovation. They include minimizing materials input, reducing energy consumption, maximizing the use of renewable sustainable resources, and extending product durability as per the World Business Council report published in 1998. Since continuous improvement of the process is helpful for mitigating the environmental damages caused by the process concept, eco-efficiency, simultaneously maximizing productivity and environmental performance can be improved as suggested by Wang, Ming, Li, Kong, Wang, Wu in their paper published in 2011.

Previous views of sustainability can be classified in three dimensions: (a) pollution prevention; (b) product stewardship, and (c) sustainable development.

Table 2.2: Dimensions of sustainability

Authors	Publication Title	Scope of paper
Ginovsky, John, 2009	Green banking	The article focuses on the efforts of community banks in the U.S. to leverage sustainability, or green banking.
British Institute of Management (BIM), 1992.	Managers urged to go green	Managers to improve the management of their environment and has launched a major report which gives basic tips on greening the workplace.
Pravakar Sahoo, Bibhu Prasad Nayak,2008.	Green banking in India	This paper explores the importance of Green Banking, sites international experiences and highlights important lessons for sustainable banking and development in India.
Jeucken, M and Bouma, J,J (1999)	The Changing Environment of Banks	Investment which take into account of environmental side-effects usually have lower rate of return in short-term.
Rutherford, Michael (1994)	At what Point can pollution be said to cause damage to the Environment?	Banks also need to monitor post transaction for the ideal environmental risk management program During the project implementation and operation.
Schmidheiny, S and Federico J L Zorraquin, (1996)	Financing Change: The Financial Community, Eco-Efficiency and Sustainable development	Commercial banking has been more attentive to the investment banking than the environmental problems; the environmental liabilities would play a larger role in their investment decision in the near future.
Gupta, S, (2003)	Do Stock market penalise Environment-Unfriendly Behaviour? Evidence from India",	The investors in the stock market are equally aware of environmental pollution and would take a stand against those industries/institutions that do not comply with pollution norms.
Ellis, BillieJ, Jr Sharon S Willians and Sandra Y Bodeau, (1992	"Helping a Lender Develop Environmental Risk Program,"	Risk of loan default by debtors due to environmental liabilities because of fines and legal liabilities and due to reduced priority of repayment under bankrupcy. In few cases, banks have been held responsible for actions occurring in which they held a secured interest.
Jeucken, M (2001)	Sustainable Finance and Banking, The finance Sector and the Future of the Planet"	The banking and financial institutions should prepare an environmental risk and liability guidelines on development of protective policies and reporting for each project they finance or invest.
Blacconiere, Walter and Dennis Pattern, (1993)	Environment Disclosure, regulatory costs and changes in firm values,"	Studies showing positive correlation between environmental

		performance and financial performance.
Hamilton, James T (1995)	"Pollution as News: Media and Stock markets Reactions to the toxics release inventory data"	Studies showing p o s i t i v e correlation b e t w e e n e n v i r o n m e n t a l performance and financial performance.
Hart, Stuart. (1995)	"Does it Pay to be green? An Empirical Examination of the relationship between Emissions Reduction and Firm Performance"	Studies showing p o s i t i v e correlation b e t w e e n e n v i r o n m e n t a l performance and financial performance.
Hall, Jeremy K., Daneke, Gregory A,Lenox, Michael J, 2010.	Sustainable development and sustainability: past contributions and future directions.	**Sustainability** has been recognized as a major conduit for **sustainable** products and processes, and new ventures are being held up as a panacea for many social and environmental concerns.
Douglas J. Lober, (1998)	"Pollution prevention as sustainability"	Pollution prevention is a new concept of the idea of environmental sustainability as it is process based and focused on reducing costs rather than increasing revenues.
Pacheco, Desirée F, Dean, Thomas J and Payne, David S (2010)	Escaping the green prison: Sustainability and the creation of opportunities for sustainable development.	In this prison, entrepreneurs are compelled to environmentally degrading behavior due to the divergence between individual rewards and collective goals for **sustainable development**.
Boks C (2006).	The soft side of ecodesign	Organizations involved in eco-design concept are generally subject to the same influencing factors. One frequently mentioned factor is management commitment and support.
Chan RY (2001).	Determinants o f Chinese consumers – g r e e n purchase behaviour.	Not only does environmental responsiveness help organizations to remain competitive and increase market share.
Chang NJ, Fong CM (2010).	Green product quality, green corporate image, green customer satisfaction, and green customer loyalty.	green product quality had positive effects on green customer satisfaction and green customer loyalty.
D'Souza C, Taghian M, Lamb P, Peretiatkos R (2006).	Green products and corporate strategy: an empirical investigation.	Not only does environmental responsiveness help organizations to remain competitive and increase market share but also there is some evidence showing increases in customer loyalty.
Lubin, David A.; Esty, Daniel C. (2010)	Green productivity indexing A practical step towards integrating environmental protection into corporate performance.	The needs for efficient use of sustainable resources and environment friendly corporate policies and behaviors have now been recognized all over.
Vitola, Alise; Senfelde, Maija (2010)	It's green, it's friendly, it's wal-mart, eco-store	Not only does environmental responsiveness help organizations to remain competitive and increase market share.
Hart SL (2005).	Innovation, creative destruction and sustainability	Green management in organizations has to go beyond regulatory compliance and needs to include conceptual tools such as pollution prevention, product stewardship a n d corporate social responsibility.
Pujari D, Peattie K, Wright G (2004).	Organizational antecedents of environmental responsiveness in industrial new product development.	One frequently mentioned factor is management commitment and support.
Saxena AK, Bhardwaj KD, Sinha KK (2003).	Sustainable g r o w t h through green productivity: a case of edible oil industry in India.	The performance of an enterprise can no longer be evaluated on the basis of economic parameters alone and it needs to be integrated with environmental performance as well.
Ritzén S (2000)	Integrating Environmental Aspects into Product Development – Proactive Measures.	One frequently mentioned factor is management commitment and support.
Khandwalla PN, Mehta K (2004).	Design of corporate creativity	In order to survive and compete successfully, the organization needs innovation-friendly business strategy, organizational structure, top management style, middle management practices and effective modes of managing innovation for innovational success and competitive excellence.

Kumar S, Putnam V (2008)	Cradle to cradle: reverse logistics strategies and opportunities across three industry sectors.	Moving towards sustainable development, therefore, is now a major concern in most of the developed countries, resulting in stricter regulations concerning the impact of the products during their manufacturing, use and end of life including the obligation to define reverse logistics strategies and systems.
Hong IH, Ammons JC, Realff MJ (2008).	Decentralized decision-making and protocol design for recycled material flows	Moving towards sustainable development, therefore, is now a major concern in most of the developed countries, resulting in stricter regulations concerning the impact of the products during their manufacturing, use and end of life including the obligation to define reverse logistics strategies and systems.
Ehrenfeld J, Lenox M (1997).	The Development and Implementation of DfE Programmes.	Organizations involved in eco-design concept are generally subject to the same influencing factors. One frequently mentioned factor is management commitment and support.
Gou Q, Liang L, Huang Z, Xu C. (2008).	A joint inventory model for an open-loop reverse supply chain.	Moving towards sustainable development, therefore, is now a major concern in most of the developed countries, resulting in stricter regulations concerning the impact of the products during their manufacturing, use and end of life including the obligation to define reverse logistics strategies and systems.

For the purpose of the research, *Internal-improvement-based GR practices* are central to minimizing emissions, effluents, and waste in operations, which in turn help companies reduce costs and gain in environmental performance. This is consistent with the philosophy of total quality environmental management (TQEM), which focuses on improving the efficiency of production, minimizing waste, and reducing costs throughout the entire corporate system. Congruent with the "zero-defects" goal of TQEM, *internal-improvement-based greening* demands continuous improvement at every step of the operations process with a view to attaining total elimination of waste.

Continuous improvement is concerned with constant evaluation and improvement of the operations process for enhancing efficiency. There are several ways to gain efficiency through process improvement and innovation. They include minimizing materials input, reducing energy consumption, maximizing the use of renewable sustainable resources, and extending product durability. Since continuous improvement of the process is helpful for mitigating the environmental damages caused by the process concept, eco-efficiency simultaneously maximizing productivity and environmental performance can be improved. Consistent with the notion of eco-efficiency that environmental impact should be reduced throughout a product's life cycle, *external-coordination-based greening processes* focuses on coordinating with related parties to minimize the life-cycle cost of the product.

2.3   INTERNAL FACTORS FOR SUSTAINABILITY

Pollution prevention is a new concept of the idea of environmental sustainability as it is process based and focused on reducing costs rather than increasing revenues. Sustainability has been recognized as a major conduit for sustainable products and processes, and new ventures are being held up as a panacea for many social and environmental concerns. While sustainable activity has been an important force for social and ecological sustainability; its efficacy is dependent upon the nature of market incentives. This limitation is sometimes explained by the metaphor of the prisoner's dilemma, which we term the green prison. In this prison, entrepreneurs are compelled to environmentally degrading behavior due to the divergence between individual rewards and collective goals for sustainable development. With two main predictors, namely, top management commitment and employee support. The effect of green development and environmental aspects as well as CSR and local community engagement on financial performance is also considered as positive, but mainly indirect through non-financial performance from the employee perspective. Not only does environmental responsiveness help organizations to remain competitive and increase market share but also there is some evidence showing increase in customer loyalty. This may be also termed as green marketing. Xu and Mirza in 2012 argued that green product quality had positive effects on customer satisfaction and customer loyalty. Green management in organizations has to go beyond regulatory compliance and needs to include conceptual tools

24

such as pollution prevention, product stewardship and corporate social responsibility. The needs for efficient use of sustainable resources and environment friendly corporate policies and behaviors have now been recognized all over (Das et al., 2006). The performance of an enterprise can no longer be evaluated on the basis of economic parameters alone and it needs to be integrated with environmental performance as well (Saxena et al., 2003). Moving towards sustainable development, therefore, is now a major concern in most of the developed countries, resulting in stricter regulations concerning the impact of the products during their manufacturing, use and end of life including the obligation to define reverse logistics strategies and systems (Gou et al., 2008; Hong et al., 2008; Kumar and Putnam, 2008). Organizations involved in eco-design concept are generally subject to the same influencing factors. One frequently mentioned factor is management commitment and support (Ehrenfeld and Lenox, 1997; Ritzén, 2000; Pujari et al., 2004; Boks, 2006). In order to survive and compete successfully, the organization needs innovation-friendly business strategy, organizational structure, top management style, middle management practices and effective modes of managing innovation for innovational success and competitive excellence (Khandwalla and Mehta, 2004).

However, recent writings on the topic appear to converge on at least eight important factors for sustainability including (i) green policy, (ii) green human sustainable resource management, (iii) green technology, (iv) green supply chain management, (v) production flexibility.

2.4.1 *Green Policy*

This study suggests that companies should invest their sustainable resources in cultivating the internal origins rather than the external origins. Discussing the information technology industry's efforts to promote green technology, Salvati and Carlucci (2011) propose that component power management could reduce climate damage and save energy without negatively impacting performance. This could be effectively enhanced by designing proper internal policy for pursuing green initiatives for reducing carbon footprints.

Moreover, other practices such as Total Quality Management; supply chains; leadership; concept of green consumers; a green version of Deming process are some of the strategic planning for green businesses (Schuller, 2011). In one of its research on green policy, Stephen (2007) studied the influence of Wal-Mart's green policy on the usage of use of imported polyethylene terephthalate (PET) in packaging. Study on the influence of green management strategy on 3Ps (people, planet and politics) proposes that Wal-Mart emphasizes its US suppliers to beta-test on environmental scorecard for packaging. Aggressive offers of Asia PET contributed to a slump in US PET prices in the fourth quarter of 2006, with India overtaking China and Thailand as the principal Asia source. The report further suggests that imports of usage of PET technology in the first 11 months of 2006 were 614,500 tonnes, up 39% from 518,000 tonnes in the year-earlier period, according to the latest government data. The environmental strategy has become the sustainable and competitive strategy of the company. There are several policies which influence the adoption of the green strategy by organizations. Some of these relate to issues such as climate change; waste; water ecosystems. For instance, Jones, Hill, Comfort and Hillier (2008) reviewed the government policies and companies' initiatives in six priority areas namely climate change; waste; water ecosystems; nutrition and obesity; and fair relationships within supply chains.

The determinants of adoption of green initiatives by the organizations are composed of technological, organizational, and environmental (TOE) dimensions. In one of the breakthrough papers, Stephen (2012) proposed that charging for carbon can inspire conservation, fuel competition, and enhance competitiveness. Moreover, the authors also suggest that environmental policies need to be carefully structured and predicted for enhancing competitiveness.

2.4.2 Green Sustainable Human resource Management

Emphasizing on sustainability as key driver of innovation, Nidumolu, Prahalad, and Rangaswami (2009) found that the quest for sustainability can lead to organizational and technological innovations that can yield both top-line and bottom-line returns for companies. These transformations may include change in the competitive landscape by redesigning products, technologies, processes, and business models. Equating sustainability with innovation, the authors further described the five distinct stages of change involved in this process: (1) viewing compliance as opportunity; (2) making value chains sustainable; (3) designing sustainable products and services; (4) developing new business models; and (5) creating next-practice platforms. However, some of the critical success factors would include the understanding of the challenges that each stage entails and defining the sustainable capabilities needed to tackle them.

Studying the foundations and capstone, core values of ethics, Heuer (2010) provided simulations as an important pedagogical tool for sustainability education. Empirical study conducted by Bhardwaj et al. (2012) shows that internal environment is very important for creating the innovative environment through sustainability. The author undertook sustainable resource review evaluated simulations of offerings ranging from stand-alone courses to modules supporting individual courses related to sustainability education. The study conducted by Bhatnagar, Bhardwaj and Gupta (2012) shows that sustainability education is very critical for women sustainability running technological business. For example studying the sustainability imperative, Lubin and Esty (2010) discussed the concepts of business megatrends and of sustainability which influence companies' capacity to create value for consumers (Bhardwaj, Sushil, Momaya; 2011a,b). Some of the critical criteria of venture investment in clean technology and sustainability programs include externalities that can affect a business' competitiveness, and the shift in consumers' preferences toward efficiency leading to Total Quality Management. Moreover, the study also identified five areas where companies must excel in sustainability are leadership, management integration, and communication.

Starik and Rands (1995) developed an integrated web to study the multisystem perspectives of ecological sustainable organizations. The authors explored the concept of ecological sustainability and applied it to organizations by utilizing a systems framework and multiple levels of analysis. The study explored the relationships between the organization and entities at the individual, organizational, political-economic, social-cultural, and ecological environment levels from ecological sustainability perspective. The study suggests the critical factors that influence the degree of ecologically sustainable behaviors of the organization. The study further examined the behavioral and structural elements of the ecologically sustainable organizations (ESOs). Studying the need for scale development in the built environment and physical infrastructure in the 'developing countries', Plessis (2007) designed a strategic framework for sustainable construction in developing or emerging countries. We will adopt ESO model to understand these variables and their correlations with the adoption of environmental friendly initiatives by the companies in India.

2.3.4 Green Production Flexibility

Production flexibility can offer a firm that has a distinctive competitive advantage, because the sustainable capabilities to generate decision-making options, and hence different forms of strategic flexibility to deal with sustainable and changing environments, is probably difficult for competitors to imitate (Salvati, and Carlucci, 2011). Zhang, Xu, Yu and Jiao (2012) examined structure indices for process flexibility planning with efficiency loss in cross production. The authors generalize the Structural Flexibility Index and the Graph Expander Index by incorporating shrinking capacity factors. These two deterministic indices are computationally tractable and they allow for simple analysis of alternative system designs. Therefore, they can help design an effective flexibility structure without extensive simulations. Numerical experiments show that both indices can predict the flexibility performance of various system structures.

The flexibility is defined as the degree of freedom given for sustainability concept including planning, identification of suppliers and implementation of plan. Flexibility is also defined as the degree of freedom of action in terms of roles and responsibilities. Three aspects characterize systemic flexibility: options, change and freedom of choice. Identification of flexibility on any plane requires delineation of the range of options (Sushil, 1993, 1994, 1997, 1999, 2000). Barret and Weinstein (1998) defined flexibility as the degree to which a business unit is adaptable in administrative relations and the authority is vested in situational expertise (Kanter, 1985; Khandwalla, 1997; Zenger and Marshall, 2000; Stajkovic and Luthans, 2001; Tettech et al., 2001). The dimension 'existence of a supportive

29

organizational structure' (Sathe, 1985; Hisrich and Peter, 1986) provides the administrative mechanisms by which ideas are evaluated, chosen and implemented (Burgelman and Sayles, 1986; Palanisamy, 2001). Other researchers have also emphasized on the appropriate organizational structure, which provides product flexibility within the organization (Brazeal, 1993). Slater and Narver (1995) proposed that a firm's market orientation is complemented by sustainability and organizational flexibility.

The development of the requisite "strategic flexibility" (Eisenhartdt and Tabrizi, 1995) in the customer intelligence development process is critical aspect of sustainability. Practicing flexibility, particularly in performance appraisal and reward systems, encourage people for risk taking and innovation (Haddad, 1996). Flexibility in organization structure contributes positively towards products success (Saleh and Wang, 1993). Graham (1995) emphasized the need to match the organic structure to a proactive management style, which facilitates good communication and the free flow of information for effective market orientation (Stopford and Baden-Fuller, 1994; Upton, 1994).

The innovation process has been described as chaotic and unpredictable (Van de Ven, 1986). Judge, Fryxell, and Dooley (1997) found that too little operating autonomy hurt innovation (Lorange, 1999). Teece (1987) has argued that entrepreneurs without authority cannot take the necessary leaps; their justifications before the fact will always turn out to be inadequate if choices are made by people who do not fully comprehend the proposals presented to them. Rosner (1968) proposed that activity control hurts innovation, but controls designed to increase the visibility of consequences help innovation. Amabile (1998) argues that people should be given freedom concerning the process but not necessarily about the ends. Dougherty and Hardy (1996) urge senior managers to build innovative organizations by 'increasing the strategic meaning of innovation', by making the concept of product innovation more meaningful to people throughout the organization. These authors have emphasized on actively and deliberately engaging in open strategic conversations around product innovation to help the "processes link the right people, sustainable resources and criteria to flow to right places". The "selected opportunity reviews" conducted by 3M provided opportunities for increasing the strategic meaning of innovation as recommended by Dougherty and Hardy (1996).

The use of "boundaryless" cross-functional new product development teams with good market input from both customers and non-customers helps to create robust product designs that do not need to be reworked in later stages of development after substantial sustainable resources have been expended in development and production. This can make it more flexible so that the supply chain can be monitored accordingly with least environmental emission. In general, shifting the relative allocation of time, effort, and sustainable resources toward the early phases of new product development reduces the overall cost and development time which translates to increased cumulative profit for the new product.

2.4.4   Green technology management (GTM)

Siegel (2011) proposed that it would be beneficial for the firms to adopt "green technology" (through CSR) only if it succeeds in yielding more green economic output in terms of better performance of the company. On the other hand, Melville (2010) studied the information systems innovation for environmental sustainability and found that information systems (IS) plays an important role in shaping beliefs about the environment and in enabling and transforming sustainable processes and practices in organizations. On the basis of the research, the author developed a belief--action--outcome (BAO) framework and associated research agenda provided the basis for a new perspective on IS for environmental sustainability.

On the contrary, green practice's complexity and environmental uncertainty influences the green practice adoption negatively. Similarly, due to increasing ecological pressures from a variety of institutional players such as market, governmental, and competitive sources, some players from the Chinese manufacturing industry have initiated green supply chain management (GSCM) practices (Zhu and Sarkis, 2007). On the basis of a moderated hierarchical regression analysis of 341 Chinese manufacturers revealed that the environmental pressure on Chinese manufacturers to implement GSCM practices are increasing. Moreover, the study also shows that existence of market (normative) and regulatory (coercive) pressures influence the environmental performance of organizations and enhance the adoption of eco-design and green purchasing practices. The study further shows that higher regulatory pressures influence the decision to implement green purchasing and investment recovery.

Similarly, Gonzalez-Benito (2008) studied 184 companies from three industrial sectors, and verified that organizational attribute such as manufacturing pro-activity is a good predictor of environmental pro-activity and environmental pro-activity is one of the distinguishing characteristics of the companies which is governed by the operations function. While reviewing of green supply chain management (GSCM), Sarkis, Zhu, and Lai (2011) categorized GSCM literature under nine broad organizational theories, and emphasized on investigation of adoption, diffusion and strategy of GSCM practices. Similarly, working on the sustainable framework of "green" specification for construction in Hong Kong, Lam,

32

Chan, Chau and Poon (2011) proposed a green specification framework which can be effective contractual tool to help achieve green construction by modeling after established green specification systems. Some of the important specifications of the tools include time, cost, quality and liability. On the basis of series of interviews with construction stakeholders, three sample work sections of green specification was prepared for concrete, paint and lighting representing structural, architectural and building services. The study shows that in Hong Kong, quality of construction is perceived to be good if the specific framework mentioned above is adopted. The study further proposes a roadmap for its sustainable adoption. Similarly, assessing the financial returns from green structural and infrastructural expenditures, Klassen and Biehl (2009) studied the range of management decisions, programs and technologies that contribute to greener operations. This study identified some of the strategic sustainable resources such as infrastructural expenditures related to assessments, monitoring, auditing, administering environmental programs, and environmental training. On the basis of Canadian government databases, the study found that increasing expenditures on and allocating a greater allocation toward management practices yields positive financial returns across several specific cost and inventory metrics (Ahuja and Lampert, 2001; Burnett and Hansen, 2008; Arrow, 1980; Bandura, 1986).

The emphasis on information and communication technology (ICT) has boosted investments in research and developments as well as Internet penetration and literacy rates. The emergence of technological innovations has opened up to new opportunities and challenges to businesses. Lalkaka (2002) defined technological innovation as the process that drives a concept towards a marketable product or service. This holds true as it contributes towards raising productivity and competitiveness. In this regard, technological adoption and

33

advancement act as channel to expand and accelerate the businesses as well as the people. Businesses will be able to expand themselves to compete in this borderless world, at the same time create, and add value to their business in order to achieve sustainability.

The rapid advancement of technology has encouraged small and medium-sized businesses (SMEs) to utilize the opportunity to establish, expand, as well as prosper their businesses. Extensive involvement of SMEs in generating revenue to the nations have shown that they are capable of generating employment opportunities, mobilizing the local sustainable resources, creating a balanced and affluent society and playing a significant complementary role to large firms and eventually strengthening the economic development of the nation as a whole (APEC, 2001). However, the brisk movement of technology has not always been good for some. This is because those who are already strong are prospering and others falling behind. As such, it is important for SMEs to plan their business carefully so that the changes in the technology and environment will always bring in positive returns.

O'sullivan and Shefrin (2002) defined sustainable ability as the human sustainable resources that combine the other sustainable resources such as land, labour and capital to produce a product, make non-routine decisions, innovative and bear risks. Sustainability is a field studied by economist, psychologists, and sociologists whose paths rarely cross (Leibenstein, 1987). Stevenson et al. (1990) defined sustainability as the pursuit of opportunity with regard to sustainable resources currently controlled. Drucker (1985), a management theorist notes that entrepreneurs see change as the norm and as healthy and they always search for change, respond to it and exploit it as an opportunity. In simple term, Drucker, (1985) believed that entrepreneurs act as agents of change and defined entrepreneurs as individuals that create a new market with a new customer.

This motion is supported by Schumpeter (1947), an economist in Miller and Friesen (1983) that "…the entrepreneur and his function are not conceptualize: the defining characteristic is simply the doing new things or doing of things that are already being done in new way (innovation)…". These innovations can be in the forms of new products, new production methods, new markets or new forms of organization. Innovation is the tool all entrepreneurs utilize across their environments and exploitation of change is firmly rooted in innovation (Yarzebinski, 1992). Quite often, entrepreneurs form small new companies called start-ups: firms focused on creating and introducing a particular new product or employing a specific new production or distribution technique. By adopting new technologies in an inherent organized, purposeful, systematic manner, the entrepreneur innovates (Yarzebinski, 1992).

Various literatures use the term "technology-based entrepreneurs", "technical entrepreneurs", "high technology entrepreneurs" or even "high tech new ventures" to describe new business that combine sustainable skills and technology (Oakey, 2003; Kakati, 2003). For instance, the United States emphasizes labels like high tech small firm or new technology-based firm for venture business while Japan legally recognizes new ventures as a firm that invest more than 3% of total sales in R&D (Sung et al. 2003). Other example includes technical entrepreneur, who originally trained as professional engineers but instinctively taught him or her to become expert business managers (Oakey, 2003). Technology-based entrepreneur is a process and formation of a new business that involves technology and these "technopreneurs" use technological innovations and translate such technology into successful products or services. Based on this perspective, the culture of innovation as discussed in the earlier section was nurtured but in this case, it is more focused on technological innovation.

2.4.5   Green supply chain management (GSCM)

Routroy (2009) analyzed the factors which influences the adoption of green practices in Chinese logistics industry and found the determinants are composed of technological, organizational, and environmental dimensions. The authors surveyed the green technology adopted by Chinese logistics companies. The sample size of 322 revealed that the various factors such as organizational support, relative advantage and compatibility of green practices, regulatory pressure, quality of human sustainable resources, and governmental support influences the adoption of green practices for Chinese logistics companies. In one of its sustainable development initiatives, Bharti Wal-Mart launched a potentially groundbreaking initiative to measure suppliers' energy use. In this study, Herbst and Moira (2007) studied how Bharti Wal-Mart balances the green of the environment with the green of its balance sheet. The study suggests that companies can have a huge impact given its sheer size and power. The study further revealed Bharti Walmart's plans to enhance the fuel economy of its trucks by 2015 which would save 60 million gallons of diesel fuel a year. One of the company's pledge is to make its stores 20% more energy efficient by 2013 which would cut annual electricity use by 3.5 million mega-watt hours. And by Bharti Wal-Mart's estimates, if each of its 100 million-plus customers bought one long-lasting compact fluorescent light bulb, that would reduce electric bills by $3 billion, conserve 50 billion tons of coal, and keep 1 billion incandescent light bulbs out of landfills over the life of the bulb. Heather Rogers, author of Gone Tomorrow: The Hidden Life of Garbage, argues that it would have been more meaningful to focus on other products that typically do require carbon emissions including cell phones and DVD players, and developing technologies for managing electronic waste (E-Waste Management System).   Similarly, using Japanese facility-level data, authors have found that ISO 14001 certification promotes the green supply chain management (GSCM) practices. The study also revealed that facilities with environmental management systems (EMS) certified by ISO 14001 help to assess the suppliers" environmental performance and influences the decision about adoption of environmental practices. Also, it is seen from the study results that government programs encourage voluntary EMS adoption and promotes GSCM practices.

By 2013 Wal-Mart will be offsetting its cut of 2.5 million metric tons of carbon dioxide by adding 28 million metric tons of new emissions within the same time period. According to Gogoi and Moira Herbst (2008), Meijer Inc. has opened a store with a fresh unit that incorporates a number of sustainability innovations located in Battle Creek, Michigan. The new store is the company's replacement from its testing of green operations in Monroe. Pledging to cooperate with its suppliers to lessen the environmental impact of its operations in Great Britain, Wal-Mart launched the "Sustainability 360" program to make its customers and suppliers greener. The firm also introduced a new ethical-sourcing initiative in 2007.

In the current time development in every field has become a crucial part, as the environmental concerns are growing and environmental rules and norms are clutching to the necks of developers, so new green methods are being devised out. In today's competitive market success of the a company is based on pillars of environmental and social actions non only limited to the company's functioning but also of that of its suppliers and related people.(Accenture, 2008). Before understanding the sustainable development any further we need to understand the meaning of this widely used term.

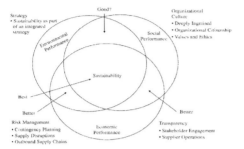

FIGURE Source: Carter and Easton (2011: 48)

Sustainable development refers to the development for meeting the needs of the current generation but at the same time keeping in mind that while fulfilling our present need we don't forget about our future generation concluding this broad definition into one line we can say that "Sustainable development is development that meets the needs of the present without compromising the ability of future generations to meet their own needs" (Brundtland, 1987).

Now that we have gathered an understanding about the term sustainable development by the definition and diagram depicted above we need to firstly analyze the need for which this type of development came up. The year 2010 was recorded for the highest greenhouse gas emissions. Even the environmentalist have not been able properly able to analyze the implication of the emissions properly, yet concerns over this matter have considerably risen due to the research which has stated a total of 2 degree rise in global middle temperature or what we call a average temperature due to the amount of emissions continue to flood the clean air and establishing a suffocating environment and bringing about a dangerous/drastic climate change which will become an obstacle in smooth flow of human life (Harvey, 2011). Concerns over this matter rose even more when chances for water and food insecurity aroused. It might even worsen the situation by creating a wider gap in the uneven distribution of sustainable resources or even exhaustion in few areas now inhabited, while other places would flourish. This situation would lead to mass migration or even conflicts on a whole disrupting the smooth flow of ecological system.

It is not always that companies are cooperative in adapting to these GREEN processes it can be either due to cost reasons or others, the judiciary, stakeholders, consumers, economic and regulatory pressures have four cornered the companies to manage their environmental and social issues. Countries like china are also being threatened by developed countries for following sustainable and environmental friendly norms (Carter and Easton, 2011; Srivastava and Srivastava, 2006; Zhu et al, 2005).

As the consequences of this human concept were analyzed the main focus came on the causes for these emissions. According to a research on carbon disclosure project's conducted in 2011 supply chain was seen as a concern area for giving a sustainable approach. It was stated that 50 percent of an average corporate emissions from the supply chain so it emerged as a vital part to enhance the entire system and giving it an environmental approach or soundness. Choosing a green supply chain by an organization can either be because of law or to give it a competitive edge in this cut throat challenge market. Law and order authorities of EU countries are playing a vital role in environmental concerns, for e.g. the government of Germany enforced many laws on German car makers which entitled them accountable for proper recycling of disposed of cars, some of these laws were German Recycling and Waste

Control Act, even US is using tax credits and various other means to promote reuse and recycling (Lapide, 2008; Nie, Xiong, Liao, 2012).

Supply chain refers to process which initiates with the intake of raw materials at the end providing us finished goods in hand through a proper well defined process. With the rising environmental many terms have originated like Green supply chain, Sustainable supply chain etc. Even if organisation agrees upon setting up of a SSCM it is not a cup of tea, it is not only costly and time consuming but also requires compliance to enormous number of standards and regulations (Anker Rasch og Sorgard, 2011).

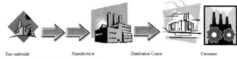

Raw materials   Manufacturer   Distribution Center   Customer

Source: Supply Chain Definitions.com, 2011

2.5   VARIABLES IDENTIFIED FROM LITERATURE SURVEY

The firm level sustainability issues having dominant influence on strategy as supported by multiple research evidences from the literature have been identified for empirical investigation under the study. Variables having similarity of concepts, or those contributing to the same result(s), have been grouped together in terms of macro variables. These antecedents are listed below:

(a) *Green policy*

Measured by (i) Explicit definition of environmental policy (ii) clear objectives and long term environmental plans (iii) objectives for reducing green house gas emission (Lai, Chen and Tang, 2010).

40

(b) Green Human Sustainable resource Management

Measured by (i) well-defined environmental responsibilities, (ii) full-time employees devoted to environmental management, (iii) natural environment training programmes for managers and employees (Lai, Chen and Tang, 2010).

(c) Green technology management

Measured in terms of (i) disposable disposal of waste and residues, (ii) acquisition of clean technology/equipment, (iii) emission filters and end-of-pipe control, (iv) enhancing water and energy conservation and (v) adoption of technology that reduces green house gas emission (Lai, Chen and Tang, 2010).

(d) Green supply chain management

Measured by (i) systems for measuring and assessing environmental performance, (ii) periodic elaboration of environmental reports, (iii) regular voluntary information about environmental management to customers and institutions, (iv) selection of cleaner transportation methods, and (v) selection of suppliers on the basis of reduction in emission (Lai, Chen and Tang, 2010).

a) Green Production flexibility

Measured by (i) freedom to develop ideas, (ii) flexibility in product planning and control focused on reducing waste, (iii) enhancing water and energy conservation (Lai, Chen and Tang, 2010).

b) Sustainability control

Measured in terms of (i) systems for measuring and assessing environmental performance, (ii) product planning and control focused on reducing waste, (iii) periodic elaboration of environmental reports (Lai, Chen and Tang, 2010).

2.6 CONCLUDING REMARKS

The study shows the importance of organizational sustainability to society and of ESOs generally, with respect to various management theories and to interactions at the organizational level of analysis. Through this chapter we aim to promote the idea that companies in India should consider expanding this theory-connecting effort and examining their own practices to identify opportunities for advancing sustainable technopreneurship on an on-going basis, including through the use of eco-friendly initiatives such as green product and others.

The study also shows that Indian sustainability practices would be benefited by establishing green policy to orient the employees towards the techno innovation. Further, companies would also enhance the performance of the organization by reviewing the retailer's environmental impacts through GSCM initiatives. Analyzing the respondents' best practices, we found that green strategy comprising of green policy, green technology, and green human sustainable resource could be implemented by companies for better green management. Therefore the green strategy would enhance the sustainability of the techno enterprises.

CHAPTER 3

CONCEPTUAL FRAMEWORK AND EVOLUTION OF RESEARCH PLAN*

3.1 INTRODUCTION

This chapter outlines the conceptual model of sustainability and its organizational antecedents. The model is intended to depict the internal drivers of sustainability. In this research, sustainability strategy are measured in terms of the reduction of emissions, ecological, social and environmental strategy of the sustainability efforts. A conceptual model has been built that captures the organizational antecedents impacting sustainability. All of these variables are controllable by management. Practice application of this research can help to create an environment for stimulating adoption of sustainability.

3.2 CONCEPTUAL FRAMEWORK FOR THE STUDY

3.2.1 Components of the Model and their Interrelationships

Sustainability is a process whereby an individual or group adopts or undertakes actions with social, economic and environmental strategy in mind. Sustainability is defined as, "Meeting the needs of the present without compromising the ability of the future generations to meet their own needs" (Burndtland Commission, WECD, 1997:8). Sustainability has three pillars; namely, social, economic, and environmental (SEE Model) (Elkington, 1998; Schmidheiny, 2002; Rondinelli & Berry, 2000). Policy plays an important role in enhancing the adoption of sustainable practices.

*Part of this chapter has been published as:
Bhardwaj, B.R. (2012) Green Innovations for the Future Transport: SAP-LAP Framework of Analysis, chapter published in a book edited by Dr. Noopur Khosla, on Sustainable Development in India, Himalaya Publications, India.

Moreover, study found that Wal-Mart's sustainable policy has positive influence on the usage of polyethylene terephthalate (PET) in packaging. Due to this policy, there is a positive influence of sustainable management strategy (3Ps: people, planet and politics) on enhancing environmental scorecard. According to Gogoi and Moira Herbst (2008), Meijer Inc. has opened a store with a fresh unit that incorporates a number of sustainability innovations located in Battle Creek, Michigan. The new store is the company's replacement from its testing of sustainable operations in Monroe.

Green policy is defined as the capacity of the organization to develop missions and visions on green commitment. This behavior helps the organization to pursue sustainable pursuits.

Green Human Sustainable resource Development promotes employee participation for green development.

Green Technology Development enhances the support research, investment or co-operation with other agencies for developing technology to reduce environmental impact.

Green Product flexibility explains the degree of autonomy provided to the workers in terms of decision making related to cooperation with suppliers in designing products with environmental considerations.

Lai, Cheng and Tang (2010) identified three strategic sustainable capabilities, namely pollution prevention, product stewardship, and sustainable development. Pollution prevention takes place by improving efficiency by minimizing emissions, effluents, and waste in operations. It takes place in internal concept, operations, and logistics. The key party

44

involved is the employee. Pollution prevention can be enhanced by internal improvement of the processes.

3.3 PROBLEM CONCEPTUALIZATION

The review of literature indicates that appropriate firm-level practices facilitate the availability of internal sustainable resources and expertise to address the issues of sustainability.

3.3.1 Problem Attributes

Every research problem is a unique one for which it may not be possible for the researcher to adopt one particular research method. However, research methodology can be evolved by integrating two or more methods. Segregation and disaggregation of the attributes is important in such cases. The problem identified for this study is set in a unique situation dominated by the organization structure.

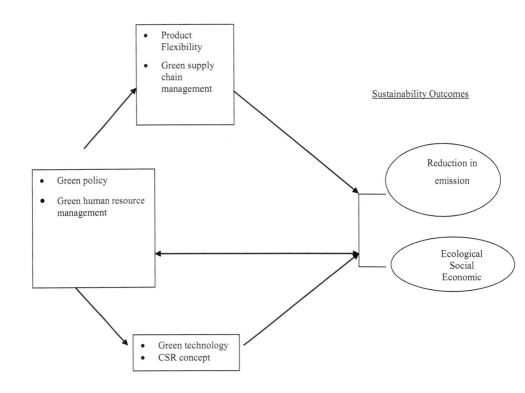

Figure 3.1: Conceptual Framework

Organizational antecedents involve the risk-taking, management support, rewards, organizational flexible boundary, work discretion, intelligence generation, green policy, and time availability for sustainability. This shows the multidimensional nature of problem, encompassing multitude of issues differing from each other in nature and also in complexity. This provided deep insight into the nature and demand of the problem and helped to evolve appropriate methodology to study and analyze the problem. The problem is complex and largely unstructured, dealing with problem situation in the strategic areas having high degree of uncertainty of outcome and therefore high level of organizational risk. It concerns the top, middle and operation level management calling for fair degree of organizational changes in the people, process and sustainable resources. The variables involved are qualitative in nature and the data/literature available for the manufacturing and service sectors is limited.

The additional variables emerging from the case study (chapter four) have also been included. To avoid repetition of table these have been marked with asterisk (*) sign in the table. The mapping is done on the basis of the interviews. The respondents were asked to rate these factors on the scale of one to ten. The overall mapping is done on the basis of aggregate rating. Based on the detailed literature review and the continua study, the various sustainability variables for investigation in the study have been identified (see Table 3.1). These variables have been measured with the help of scales developed by different researchers.

The definitions of different variables for the purpose of this study are placed at Appendix–I. These variables have been used for data collection for the questionnaire based survey study and also for the case studies. These have also been used in the empirical testing of data. The previous studies were based on the three variables including green policy, green human sustainable resource management, green technology, production flexibility for green product development. According to the present study conducted in Indian context, we found that two more variables have played a major role in stimulating sustainability in the systems including production flexibility, and green supply chain management.

Table 3.1: Sustainability Variables for Investigation in the Study

Sustainability Areas	Measurement Variables for Investigation in the Study	Author(s)
Green policy	Measured by • Explicit definition of environmental policy • Clear objectives and long term environmental plans • Policy for reducing green house gas emission	Lai et al. (2010)
Green Human Management Devlopment	Measured by • well-defined environmental responsibilities • full-time employees devoted to environmental management • natural environment training programmes for managers and employees • adopts green human sustainable resource development practices	Sathe (2005)
Green technology	Measured by • disposable disposal of waste and residues • acquisition of clean technology/equipment • emission filters and end-of-pipe control • enhancing water and energy conservation • adoption of technology that reduces green house gas emission	Zenger and Marshall (2000); Stajkovic and Luthans (2001)
Green supply chain management	Measured by o systems for measuring and assessing environmental performance o periodic elaboration of environmental reports o regular voluntary information about environmental management to customers o selection of cleaner transportation methods	Gatewood et al. (2002)

Production Flexibility	Measured by <ul><li>work performance (in terms of time, amount, quality, and timeliness)</li><li>clarity of standards of performance</li></ul> <ul style="list-style-type:circle"><li>product planning and control</li></ul>	Palanisamy (2001)

Besides the above-mentioned variables, the study also includes two other variables including GSCM and production flexibility to reduce waste. It is also important to note that if there needs to be continuous emphasis on sustainability to make the organization sustainable in the long run.

3.4 HYPOTHESES FORMULATION

Based on the conceptual framework developed in section 3.3, the set of macro hypotheses formulated is given in Table 3.2. The micro hypotheses are formulated for each variable and are given below. The micro variables describe the macro variables which are the drivers of the sustainability process.

Table 3.2: The Macro Hypotheses for Research

Variables	Hypotheses	Hypotheses Code
Green policy	Green policy influences sustainability strategy positively.	H_{GP}
Green human sustainable resource development	Green human sustainable resource development influences sustainability strategy positively.	H_{GHRM}
Green technology	Green technology influences sustainability strategy positively.	H_{GT}
Green production flexibility	Green production flexibility influences sustainability strategy positively.	H_{GPF}
Green supply chain management	Green supply chain management influence sustainability strategy positively.	H_{GSCM}

Micro Hypotheses:

The coding of the micro hypotheses is given as E for Environmental sustainability.

Green policy

The micro hypotheses of Green policy and Environmental sustainability are given below:

H_{GPE1}: Explicit definition of environmental policy influences Environmental sustainability positively.

H_{GPE2}: Clear objectives and long term environmental plans influences Environmental sustainability positively.

H_{GPE3}: Policy for reducing green house gas emission influences Environmental sustainability positively.

Green human sustainable resource development

The micro hypotheses of Green human sustainable resource development and Environmental sustainability are given below:

H_{GHRD1}: Well-defined environmental responsibilities influences Environmental sustainability positively.

H_{GHRD2}: Full-time employees devoted to environmental management influences Environmental sustainability positively.

H_{GHRD3}: Natural environment training programmes influences Environmental sustainability positively.

Green technology

H_{GT1}: Disposable disposal of waste and residues influences Environmental sustainability positively.

H_{GT2}: Acquisition of clean technology/equipment influences Environmental sustainability positively.

H_{GT3}: Emission filters and end-of-pipe control influences Environmental sustainability positively.

H_{GT4}: Enhancing water and energy conservation influences Environmental sustainability positively.

H_{GT5}: Adoption of technology that reduces green house gas emission influences Environmental sustainability positively.

Green production flexibility

H_{GPF1}: Freedom to Develop Ideas influences Environmental sustainability positively.

H_{GPF2}: Flexibility in product planning and control influences Environmental sustainability positively.

H_{GPF3}: Enhancing water and energy conservation influences Environmental sustainability positively.

Green supply chain management

H_{GSCM1}: Systems for measuring and assessing environmental performance influences Environmental sustainability positively.

H_{GSCM2}: Periodic elaboration of environmental reports influences Environmental sustainability positively.

H_{GSCM3}: Regular voluntary information about environmental management to customers influences Environmental sustainability positively.

H_{GSCM4}: Selection of cleaner transportation methods influences Environmental sustainability positively.

The green policy, technology, and green human sustainable resource management have been studied through quantitative methodology. The green production flexibility and green supply chain management have been studied through the case study methodology.

3.5   RESEARCH METHODOLOGY

In view of the problem attributes discussed earlier in section 3.3.2 and the problem conceptualization on different continua presented in Figure 3.2, two different methodologies were adopted, namely 7S framework and principles of Flexible Systems Methodology (FSM) have been used.

The study is divided into three phases: (i) the pilot study to identify the organizational antecedents of sustainability, (ii) questionnaire study to establish relationships among organizational antecedents for sustainability (iii) case studies to verify and enrich the sustainability model. The framework of research methodology is given in Figure 3.3. The framework shows the structural variables and internal environmental variables which help motivate the sustainable concept within the company. The framework also shows the relationship between drivers of sustainability which are the given characteristics undertaken in the study. The Figure 3.3 mentioned below describes the methodology in detail. It shows the various steps taken to do the research and also shows the how the conceptual framework was developed.

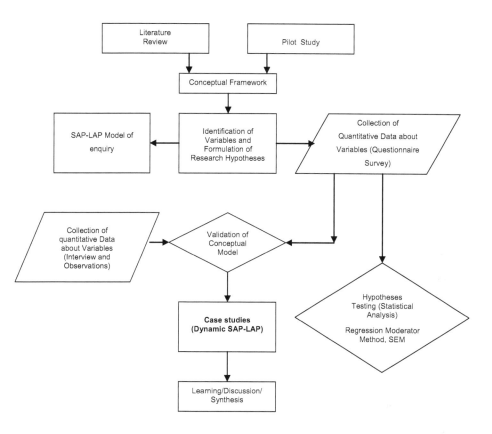

Figure 3.3: Framework of Research Methodology

3.5.1 Methodology for the Pilot Study

The empirical/pilot study aims at developing understanding about different practices of CE by organizations. Four organizations from manufacturing and services sectors were selected for the empirical study.

The data has been collected through questionnaire survey, observation and interview method and has been analyzed through SAP-LAP framework of Flexible Systems Methodology (Sushil, 1994, 1997, 2000) as presented in Figure 3.4. The issues relating to the situation, actors, and process are analyzed in the organizational context to generate/evolve learnings regarding sustainability.

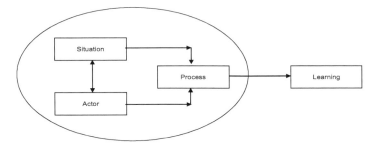

Figure 3.4: SAP Interaction for Learning

3.5.2 Methodology for the Questionnaire Study

This part of the study aims at establishing relationships between the research variables involved in the study problem. It uses questionnaire survey method, in which the unit of analysis is the firm. The questionnaire was developed and pre-tested before mailing to the selected organizations. To understand the correlation among the different variables, correlation analysis has been used. Further, to identify the difference between manufacturing and services sectors, cross case analysis has been used. Based on the conceptual model evolved in this chapter, the hypotheses have been tested statistically through stepwise multiple regression technique and the results have been synthesized to identify the organizational antecedents impacting sustainability strategy. The multivariate statistical tools are used including moderator method and structural equation modeling to identify the inter relationships between the different organizational antecedents on sustainability strategy.

3.5.3 Methodology for the Case Study

The case studies were analyzed on the basis of 7S framework developed by McKinsey. Besides, this, the case studies in sustainability were carried using SAP-LAP framework of flexible systems methodology. The learnings from the cases have been synthesized and the results were used to identify additional variables for sustainability model. Based on the findings of 7S framework, the synthesis is presented.

3.5.4 Justification of Research Methodology Chosen

As discussed in section 3.3.1, the study problem has following major attributes:

(i)   it is unstructured,

(ii)   deals with risks for the organizations,

(iii)   involves organizational change,

(iv)   set in uncertain environment

Such research problems cannot be setup in the laboratory environment through experimental methods. The field study method is also impractical as it involves large amount of time and cost. Thus, the research methods suitable for data collection include (i) survey study, (ii) observation method and (iii) case study method. However, each of these three research methods has respective merits and demerits. Observation method, if applied stand-alone way, requires considerable research in terms of cost and time. Therefore, it can only be used as a supplementary method to support/complement other main research methods. Thus, two methods are available namely survey method (questionnaire and/or interviews) and case study method. The survey method is suitable for collection of quantitative data and provides insights to the relevant issues. Therefore, the research methodology selected for this study makes optimal use of all three possibilities. Research data has been collected through carefully formulated and pre-tested mailed questionnaire to generate quantitative data for statistically testing the causal relationship among variables. The findings of the survey study are further supported and enriched by case studies where data is collected through both interview method and observation method.

3.5.5 Implementation of Research Methodology

A sample has to be true representation of population. In case of present research problem, the population or the universe is a bit ambiguous, as the detailed information about product/service/market development concept undertaken by various organizations were not available. Further, it was not practically feasible to prepare such a reliable and accurate list of organizations within reasonable cost and time.

In view of the above-mentioned facts, empirical/pilot study was carried out by selecting organizations on the basis of purposive sampling after ascertaining that the selected organizations fully qualify for inclusion in the sample. The organizations were selected on the basis of (i) number of sustainability initiatives undertaken, (ii) number of CSR concept undertaken, and (iii) sustainability index (Lai et al., 2010). The companies can be classified on the basis of location, stock ownership, market share or employees' nationality. The present study has selected the companies on the basis of the location of operation. 'Presence in the Indian market' is measured in terms of market share and its operations in the Indian market. The number of business areas in which they are present, the number of business units these organizations have, and the number of markets they serve is shown in the figures as organization structure of these organization. Out of 560 total number of manufacturing and services firms (280 manufacturing firms and 280 services firms), those firms were selected which served largest number of business areas, had largest number of business units, and were present in the largest number of markets, and were also present in Indian market. The organizations which have been selected include M&M and ABB. The selected MNEs were carrying out effective sustainable work in India. The objective of the case studies was to understand the sustainability work carried out by these organizations in India. This is demonstrated through the companies' efforts to establish its presence in large number of business areas including industries and applications. These companies have also designed the various systems, processes and structures which have helped these companies to sustain sustainability efforts. The study aimed to understand these internal environmental factors and the findings have been reported in Chapters 7 & 8.

Climate change is the most complicated issue the world is facing. Across the globe there have been continuous endeavors to measure and mitigate the risk of climate change caused by human activity. Many countries the world over have made commitments necessary to mitigate climate change. India has committed to cut its domestic carbon intensity by 20-25 percent from 2005 levels, by the year 2010. As socially responsible corporate citizens (SRCC), Indian banks have a major role and responsibility in supplementing government efforts towards substantial reduction in carbon emission. Although banks are considered environment friendly and do not impact the environment greatly through their own 'internal' operations, the 'external' impact on the environment through their customers concept is substantial. The banking sector is one of the major sources of financing industrial projects such as steel, paper, cement, chemicals, fertilizers, power, textiles, etc., which cause maximum carbon emission. Therefore, the banking sector can play an intermediary role between economic development and environmental protection, for promoting environmentally sustainable and socially responsible investment. 'Green banking' refers to the banking business conducted in such areas and in such a manner that helps the overall reduction of external carbon emission and internal carbon footprint. To aid the reduction of external carbon emission, banks should finance green technology and pollution reducing projects. Although, banking is never considered a polluting industry, the present scale of banking operations have considerably increased the carbon footprint of banks due to their massive use of energy (e.g., lightning, air conditioning, electronic/electrical equipments, IT, etc), high paper wastage, lack of green buildings, etc. Therefore, banks should adopt technology, process and products which result in substantial reduction of their carbon footprint as well as develop a sustainable business.

Caselets on Green Strategies

Various banks in India are undertaking the sustainability approach to innovate and adopt green banking strategies for sustainable development of the banks. For example, ICICI Bank India recognizes that care of the environment and the larger society in which it operates is essential both from business continuity as well as a corporate citizenship perspective. IndusInd Bank, India inaugurated Mumbai's first solar-powered ATM as part of its Green Office Project campaign 'Hum aur Hariyali'. It also unveiled a 'Green Office Manual - A Guide to Sustainable Practices', prepared in association with the Centre for Environmental Research and Education (CERE). IndusInd's new Solar ATM has replaced the use of conventional energy for eight hours per day with eco-friendly and renewable solar energy. The energy saved will be 1980 kW hrs every year and will be accompanied by a simultaneous reduction in CO_2 emissions by 1942 kgs. The uniqueness of this solar ATM is the ability to store and transmit power on demand (in case of power failure) or need (time basis). In terms of costs, the savings will be substantial, approximately Rs. 20,000 per year in case of a commercial user with grid power supply. And in areas with erratic power supply the solar will replace diesel generators and translate into savings as high as Rs. 40,200 every year.

Moreover, several banks are putting in place policies to reduce the footprint of their electrical energy consumption by implementing energy efficiency measures such as smart lighting and replacement of inefficient appliances. Additionally, they have expressed interest in procuring energy from cleaner sources if available. The majority of banks have specific policies in place to consider the environmental issues associated with energy use, purchasing, transport, recycling and waste minimization.

State Bank of India's Green Banking Policy

The State Bank of India (SBI), as part of its Green Banking Policy, will set up windmills to generate 15 MW of power in Tamil Nadu, Maharashtra and Gujarat for its own consumption. The SBI chairman inaugurated the windmills set up at Panapatti village in Tamil Nadu's Coimbatore district on April 23, 2010. The mill in Tamil Nadu will generate 4.5 MW of power, while the Maharashtra mill will have a capacity of 9 MW and Gujarat 1.5 MW. SBI was the first Bank in the country to think of generating green power as a direct substitute to polluting thermal power and implement the renewable energy project for captive use.

Citi's Equator Principles

The Equator Principles serve as a backbone for Citi's broader Environmental and Social Risk Management (ESRM) Policy, which extends beyond project finance. Citi was a leader in the development of the Equator Principles in 2003. Citi's ESRM policy was developed in 2003 and has been regularly updated to reflect implementation experience.

Infosys India Ltd. has three business units namely, services, sectors and applications. The services area is served by seven business units namely, application development and maintenance unit, corporate performance management, independent testing and validation, infrastructure management, packaged application services, systems engineering and product engineering units. The sectors area is served by aerospace and defense, automotive, banking and capital markets, communication services, discrete manufacturing, energy, healthcare, high technology, life sciences, media and entertainment, sustainable resources, transportation, utilities, and consumer packaged goods. It is present in India. This shows the large number of business areas which is one of the most important characteristics of sustainability. ICICI Bank has three business areas namely, services, sectors and products. The services area have online banking, bill payments, email wireless alerts, inter institutional transfers, wireless transfers, debit card and reward program, foreign currency and overdraft protection. The sectors area has automobile insurance, automobile finance, healthcare and consumer category. The products category has savings, certificate of deposit, credit cards, mortgages, investing, insurance, small business, student loans.

Table 3.3 presents the research methods and the sampling techniques used for various parts of the study. The unit of analysis for questionnaire study was the organization. As the information regarding the population or the universe was not fully available, the questionnaire study was carried out using snowball random sampling technique.

Table 3.3: Description of Research Methods and Sampling Techniques Used

Study Phase	Objective of the study	Research Method Used	Sampling Technique Used
Pilot study	To bring out the issues of	Case study through	Purposive

60

	sustainability	observation and interview methods	sampling
Questionnaire Study	To bring out the relationships among different variables and sustainability strategy	Questionnaire based survey method	Snow-ball random sampling
Case Study	To understand the micro issues of sustainability	Case study through observation and interview methods	Purposive sampling

Experts from different organizations and representatives of sector associations provided the names and relevant details of organizations practicing sustainability. The snowball inquiry was started from two eminent/renowned experts in this area. They in turn provided names of further experts who were consulted to identify organizations practicing sustainability. Finally, a random sample was drawn from the list of organizations practicing sustainability, prepared from this exercise. The survey-questionnaire was mailed to all organizations included in the sample. The investigations were conducted at two levels, namely (i) the firm-level (its strategy formulation, and performance), and (ii) the product or service level (Yin, 1994; 2002). Seven to ten questionnaires and SAP-LAP inquiry (Table 4.2) was administered for each case. Besides this, 58 questionnaires were collected randomly from the list of organizations prepared from the above exercise. The data collected was analyzed using statistical methods, based on standard SPSS (Statistical Package for Social Science) software package.

The questionnaire contained 35 likert-type questions that assessed the firm's internal sustainable environment. The measurement properties of questionnaire, including a factor analysis and reliability assessment were determined. The data was analyzed statically using univariate, bivariate and multivariate analyses techniques (Barret and Weinstein, 1997a, 1998). The literature suggests that managers at all levels play important roles is organizational success (Floyd and Lane, 2000; King et al., 2001; Hornsby et al., 2002; Ireland et al., 2002). Hence, the study included respondents from almost all managerial levels. During the detailed questionnaire study, 281 questionnaires were collected including respondents from 39 organizations across the country.

The case study of specific sustainability initiatives was carried out on four organizations, two from services and two from manufacturing sectors using case study method (Jain, 2005). In total, eight organizations were selected for case study analysis; four from manufacturing and four from services sectors. Out of these, four case studies (two each from manufacturing and services sectors) were undertaken at pilot study, and four (two each from manufacturing and services sectors) were taken up for detailed case study analysis. Data were collected through discussions with the managers at top, middle and operational management and through personal observations during visits to these organizations.

The cases have been analyzed using sustainable SAP-LAP (Situation-Actor-Process; Learning-Actions-Performance) framework of flexible systems management methodology. Correlation was used to examine the strength and direction of relationship between the variables (Barret and Weinstein, 1997a). Independent samples t-test and Levene's Test has been used to study the comparative analysis. Moderator method was used to study the moderating effect of more than two antecedents on sustainability outcome. Moreover, the structural equation modeling was applied to understand the inter-relationships between organizational antecedents. Finally, the synthesis has been presented as interpretive matrix (Sushil, 2005).

3.6   CONCLUDING REMARKS

The managerial practices that affect innovativeness fall into six general categories, namely, challenge, freedom, sustainable resources, work-group features, supervisory encouragement, and organizational support. To find out the links between work environment and sustainability, we have used three methodologies: experiments, interviews, and surveys. While controlled experiments allowed us to identify causal links, the interviews and surveys gave us insight into the richness and complexity of innovation within business organizations. We have studied eight organizations, and within these 281 individuals and many teams. In each research initiative, our goal has been to identify which managerial practices are definitely linked to innovative strategy and which are not. For instance, in our research, we interviewed employees from these organizations and asked them to describe in detail the most innovative events in their organizations. We then closely studied these transcripts of interviews, noting the managerial practices which created the environment – or other patterns that appeared repeatedly in the successful innovative event and, conversely, in those that were unsuccessful. Our research has also been bolstered by a quantitative survey instrument developed through pilot study. The questionnaire (appendix-II) consisted of 35 questions used to assess the internal environment of the organization, such as management support for sustainability efforts. This survey was taken by employee at top, and middle level of an organization.

For revitalization, the organizations need to pursue sustainability at business level. The study aims at understanding the antecedents of sustainability within the organization. The problem attributes have been mapped on different continua to generate in-depth understanding of the issues and to evolve appropriate research methodology for the unique nature of the research problem. The strategy dimensions of the research problems and the micro strategy variables involved therein have been identified. Based on the research evidences from the literature, a sustainability conceptual framework has been evolved. Based on this framework, research hypotheses have been formulated for statistical testing through quantitative data collected using the questionnaire survey study. The findings have been further enriched through the case studies. The research plan has also been presented. Thus, the study as a whole has been divided into three parts. Questionnaire study was done through survey and pilot and micro variables' were studied through case studies. The next chapter presents the pilot study.

CHAPTER 4

SURVEY ON PRACTICE OF SUSTAINABILITY

4.1   INTRODUCTION

The study aims at establishing the relationships between the research variables identified through the literature survey and enriched by the pilot study of the two organizations. The objective is to study the organizational antecedents of sustainability. This study is based on taking a sample, representative of the population and studying the characteristics of the sample to understand the population.

The study used questionnaire method, in which the unit of analysis is the individual firm adopting sustainable practices. The questionnaire means "a set of questions developed in an organized and ordered manner for gaining information from the people in relation to a given problem" (Thakur, 1993). It represents "conversion of statements or theory into sample questions for operationalizing the variables into the process of social research". This chapter presents questionnaire design, validation, pre-testing and administering the sample selected for the study. It also presents univariate analysis of the data collected through the questionnaire survey method.

4.2   DESIGN OF QUESTIONNAIRE

The questionnaire is "basically a collection of questions that fit the research topic and its objectives, and the answers to which will provide the data necessary to test the hypotheses formulated for the study" (Kothari, 1985).

The foundations of all questionnaires are the questions or statements for which the researcher intends to seek answer or opinion in terms of agreement (Nachmias and Nachmias, 1981).

The development of questionnaire is an exercise that involves various phases starting from clear definition of the research topic, issue identification and relationship of variables. Framing of questions need a deep understanding of the subject matter (Yin, 2002). Therefore, the questionnaire has been designed on the basis of the conceptual model presented in chapter three, using research variables identified through the literature survey and enriched through the pilot study. It uses structured questions where the respondents do not have to write their comments or replies, but have to select one of the reply options (given in the questionnaire), which matches most with their view/experience. The questions have been framed in easy language normally used by the respondents so that these are easily understandable. The questions have been framed in a manner that the question conveys only one 'thought' at a time. The language used is concrete and conforms as much as possible to the thinking of sustainability professionals in the sector. The sequence of the questions in the questionnaire have been evolved carefully, starting with general and easy questions, slowly switching to more specific questions asking for respondent's views on in-depth situation relating to the study.

Questionnaire also aims to measure the study variables to analyze testing of the hypotheses. The study involves qualitative variables. Therefore, the plan of measurement is based on qualitative assessment of the magnitude of the variables on comparative basis. Likert type scale has been used for measurement of variables where a respondent is asked to express his/her position on a scale, which has two extremes opposite to each other. The respondent is provided with reply options on the continua composed by the two extremes, on a scale of 1-7, with options including '7=strongly agree' to '1=strongly disagree'. With the assumption that equal intervals on the scale indicate equal measures of the property/variable, the scale may be assumed to be approximately close to the 'interval scale' (Kothari, 1985 and Thakur, 1993). The interval scale facilitates use of statistical measures like mean and standard deviation. Product moment correlation technique, t-test and F-test are also appropriate in the case of interval scale (Kothari 1985).

During interactions with the professionals from various organizations (during snowball inquiry, pilot study, questionnaire validation and pre-testing stages), it emerged that CE was still new to most of the firms. These firms generally adopted only some practices (not all), as identified in this study, in a particular situation. The number of sustainable measures undertaken by various organizations, where all 'areas' are exploited, may not be very large. However, it would not be possible, in a short time, to identify and list all such concept, to constitute the 'universe' of the 'population' for the study. Therefore, it would be practically very difficult to get a representative sample of such organizations, when the 'universe' itself is not defined/known. Hence, keeping in mind the objectives of the study, the set of questions in various dimensions have been designed in independent study areas. Questions have been framed to measure the variables in the particular study areas and also their influence on sustainability.

The questionnaire also contains some control questions, which may indicate the reliability of the respondents. Few questions similar to those asked in earlier parts/sections are asked again in different context(s) to introduce crosscheck(s) on the respondents' reliability. Brief description of the objective of the study and directions with respect to filling up the questionnaire are given along with the questionnaire. Further, brief directions regarding selection of the reply option(s) are given at the end of each page of the questionnaire for ease of reference. In addition, the physical appearance of the questionnaire and quality of the paper and the printing have been given due care to make it appealing to the respondents.

4.3 VALIDATION OF THE QUESTIONNAIRE

Validity of a questionnaire refers to the degree to which we are "measuring what we think we are measuring". Insufficient, validity means a research error when the research design is not able to accomplish what is set out to do. High degree of validity reflects the accurate approximation to the real value.

4.3.1 Face Validity

Face validity refers to the degree of fit/matching between the researcher's perception and the concept of the variables, which are operationalized through the questionnaire. The operational definition looks on the face of the questionnaire as though it measures the concept study. To establish face validity of the questionnaire, 12 experts were selected as judges, of whom six were the senior experienced academicians/researchers and six were senior/experienced professionals from the sector. Each judge was requested to specify his/her perception of the research variables and also indicate whether the operational definitions of the variables correspond to the concepts. During these sessions, number of definitions was written and refined and constructs were worked out. It facilitated in reaching an agreement on the attributes of a variable and framing true perception into the commonly understandable language. Thus, operational definitions of the variables were discussed number of times through multiple contextual frameworks to arrive at simple, complete and correct language/expression. As a result, the language/wording of the questions included in the questionnaire was revised through a number of validation sessions.

4.3.2 Criterion Related Validity

Criterion related validity refers to the degree to which the measurements with the questionnaire are meaningfully related to the objectives of the questionnaire. This validation was done with active involvement of 12 experts, including six senior experienced academicians/researchers and six senior/experienced professionals from the sector. Their suggestions for improvements were incorporated into the instrument/questionnaire. Wherever required, the language/wording of the questions was also corrected/refined.

4.3.3 Content Validity

Content validation is guided by the question: "Is the content of this measure representative of the content or the universe of content of the property being measured?" (Kerlinger, 1973). Content validation consists essentially in judgment. For this purpose, 12 experienced sustainability experts from the sector and academics were selected as judges and were given the questionnaire along with the objectives of the study and the operational definitions of the variables. The judges gave their expert views on two aspects, firstly, which questions measured which variable; and secondly, which objectives were being addressed in the questionnaire and which aspects of the objectives were not being covered well by the questionnaire. Wherever such problems were noticed, the text of the question(s) was modified. Some questions were altogether framed again, and some were split into separate questions for the purpose of clarity and/or completeness of inquiry/measurement. The judges also guided in re-sequencing of the questions and in framing of the control questions for crosschecking the reliability of the respondents.

4.4   QUESTIONNAIRE FORMAT

The questionnaire has been designed to cover organizational antecedents of sustainability for the study. The list of sources for questionnaire development is given in Table 4.1.

Table 4.1: List of Sources for Questionnaire Development

Construct	Source
Green policy (GP)	Adapted from Lai et al. (2010)
Green human sustainable resource management (GHRM)	Adapted from Lai et al. (2010)
Green technology (GT)	Adapted from Lai et al. (2010)
Green supply chain mgmt (GSCM)	Adapted from Lai et al. (2010)
Green production flexibility (TA)	Adapted from Lai et al. (2010)

The questionnaire used for the purpose of the study is divided into five independent study parts for different dimensions namely Green policy, Green human sustainable resource management, Green technology, Green supply chain mgmt, Green production flexibility.

Table 4.2: Study Variable Areas and Corresponding Parts of the Questionnaire

S.No.	Study Variable Areas	Number of Questions
1.	Green policy	1-6
2.	Green human sustainable resource management	7-11, 23
3.	Green technology	32-37
4.	Green supply chain mgmt	24-31
5.	Green production flexibility	15-22

Table 4.2 indicates study areas, questionnaire section parts, and number of questions in various sections/parts. The questionnaire has 35 questions to which responses were sought. In addition, demographic information was also requested from the respondent

71

separately in terms of a brief schedule at the top of the questionnaire. It was optional for the respondents to give the name, age, name/address of the organization and the designation. However, each respondent was requested to indicate the total work experience and years of experience in the current organization. Respondents were also asked to indicate the gender, i.e. male or female.

4.5 QUESTIONNAIRE TESTING

On completion of questionnaire validation, it was subjected to pre-testing through a pilot survey administered to a small sample of respondents (58 respondents). In pre-testing, respondents are selected from same population from which the actual survey studies to be made and the questionnaire is applied on it (Thakur, 1993).

4.5.1 Pre-testing

The objective of the pre-testing was to ensure that the questionnaire was easy to understand to the respondents, and to eliminate the possibilities of misunderstanding, confusion and bias. In the pre-testing, 58 respondents from services and manufacturing organizations were given the questionnaire. Later, each respondent was interviewed on the basis of the questionnaire, with an objective to locate the weak points of the questionnaire. Each respondent was requested to communicate the difficulties faced in filling up the questionnaire and possibilities for further improvements for easy understanding of respondents. The suggestions regarding language, formulation of questions, sequencing, formatting etc. were noted and further discussed in the group setting. The confusing and problem questions were reformulated in consultation with the respective respondents and rechecked with all respondents collectively. Thus, the questionnaire was edited to ensure that the content, form, sequence of questions, spacing, arrangement and physical appearance of the questionnaire are checked for getting the desired response from persons filling the questionnaire. The final version of the questionnaire is placed at Appendix-II.

4.5.2 Construct Validity

Construct validation and empirical scientific inquiry are closely allied. It does not seek to validate the test, but aims to validate the theory behind the test (Kerlinger, 1973). A measure is said to possess construct validity to the degree that it confirms to predict correlation with other theoretical prepositions. Almost all the items for various constructs for organizational antecedents have been taken from scales developed by various authors. However, some of the variables have been adapted for the research objective. Hence, the construct validity is being checked for organizational antecedents and CE outcome variables.

Factor analysis is a method for determining the number and nature of the underlying variables among larger number of measures (Kerlinger, 1973). It facilitates understanding of the structure of a correlation matrix. In particular, it allows studying the correlations among a large number of interrelated quantitative variables by grouping the variables into new factors. The variables within each factor are more highly correlated with variables in that factor than the variables in other factors.

The factorial validity helps in confirming whether the data collected for a certain set of measures do or do not reflect the latent constructs. Principle component factor analysis considers only the common variance associated with a set of variables (Kerlinger, 1973). Usually, the initial factor extraction doesn't give interpretable factors. Rotation makes larger loading even larger and smaller loadings even smaller. Therefore, process of rotation provides factors that can be named and interpreted. Though quartmax orthogonal rotation solution is analytically simpler than the varimax solution, varimax rotation has been used as it provides clearer separation of factors (Dhillon and Goldstein, 1984). While performing the construct validity, loading for entire construct has been checked.

Factor Analysis for Organizational Antecedents and Sustainability Strategy

The principal component factor analysis has been used to test the construct validity of organizational antecedents and the Sustainability strategy. In the extraction method of principal component factor analysis, ten factors with eigen values greater than 1.0 collectively explaining 94.16 per cent of variance have been retained after varimax rotation. Table 4.3 presents the factor analysis for organizational antecedents and Sustainability strategy. It is seen from the table that there are five variables which have shown loading including Green policy, Green human sustainable resource management, Green technology, Green supply chain mgmt, Green production flexibility on Environmental sustainability. The confirmatory factors retained for organizational antecedents and sustainability strategy are presented in Table 4.4. The factor loadings for different constructs are given in Appendix IV.

Table 4.3: Factor Analysis for Organizational Antecedents and Sustainability Strategy

Factor	Factor Name	Eigen Value	Per cent of Variance	Cumulative Per cent
1	Green policy	10.958	15.219	48.022
2	Green human sustainable resource management	7.096	9.856	72.204
3	Green technology	2.782	3.864	87.916
4	Green supply chain mgmt	1.491	2.070	92.116
5	Green production flexibility	1.472	2.045	94.161

It is seen that all variables, as originally envisaged, are included in the constructs Green policy, Green human sustainable resource management, Green technology, Green supply chain mgmt, Green production flexibility. The macro variable green production flexibility shows loading on environmental sustainability. These items have been included in the respective constructs. Thus, the confirmatory factor analysis of the organizational antecedents and sustainability strategy confirms the validity of these organizational antecedents' and sustainability strategy constructs. These items have been included in the final questionnaire for survey study.

4.5.3 Reliability Assessment

Internal consistency reliability measures were assessed on the factor structures derived from both analyses reported above, using the Chronbach's procedure available in the SPSS statistical package. Those variables have been retained for which the values of Chronbach alpha are more than 0.5 (Table 4.5).

Table 5.5: Reliability Assessment

Variables	Cronbach Alpha
Green policy	0.76
Green technology	0.76
Green human sustainable resource management	0.79
Green supply chain management	0.60
Green production flexibility	0.83

5.6   ADMINISTERING THE QUESTIONNAIRE

The questionnaire has been administered with a brief write-up on the study objectives, purpose of the questionnaire survey and directions regarding filling up the questionnaire. The questionnaire was mailed along with a covering letter from the researcher and a self-addressed stamped envelope for sending the filled questionnaire back to the researcher. The unit of analysis for the study is the firm.

An ideal sample has to be true representation of population. In case of present research problem, the population or the universe was not defined, as there was no ready-made compilation of organizations undertaking corporate sustainable efforts. Further, it was practically not feasible to prepare such a reliable and accurate list of organizations practicing sustainability.

As the information regarding the population or the universe was not available, the questionnaire study was carried out using snowball sampling. Generally, this sampling is considered a non-probability sampling technique. Some authors have developed a methodology for making the approach closer to probabilistic sampling, in which one should draw a random sample, either within each stage or out of total snowball items (Baily, 1993). Eminent technologists, academicians, senior technical representatives of all sectors and experts were approached under 'snowball inquiry', with request to provide the names and relevant details of organizations undertaking sustainability practices, who qualify for inclusion into the sample for this study.

The snowball inquiry was started from two eminent/renowned experts in sustainability research and two in sector practices. These respondents provided the names of experts who may be consulted to identify organizations adopting sustainability strategy. Collection of snowball units up to this stage was purposive in nature. It provided names of 560 organizations, from service and manufacturing organizations, practicing sustainability strategy in some way or the other. Out of this list, a random sample of 380 was drawn. The survey-questionnaire was mailed to all the 380 organizations included in the sample, requesting them to fill up the questionnaire. 49 organizations responded to the questionnaire. In total, 281 responses were received. The general consensus on sample size for generalizability was (Hair et al., 1998): there should be five observations for each independent variable. The independent variables in the research are eight, so sample size should be at least 40 (5 for each variable). Considering the focus of the book on select organizations, the sample of 181 is considered adequate (even if we go to desirable ratio between 15 to 20 suggested in books (Hair et al., 1998). The sector-wise responses received are given in Table 4.6.

Table 4.6: Sector-wise Break-up of the Respondent Organization

Sector	No. of Organizations	No. of Responses	Per cent of the Respondents
Manufacturing	16	73	40.33
Service	23	108	59.67
Total	39	181	100

Table 4.6 indicates that 40.33 per cent responses are from manufacturing and 59.67 per cent responses are from service sector. The total experience-wise and region-wise break-up of responses is given in Tables 4.7 and 4.8 respectively.

Table 4.7: Region-wise Break-up of the Responses Received

Region	Responses (per cent)
North	35
East	27
West	24
South	14
Total	100

Table 4.8: Managerial Level-wise Break-up in the Current Organization of the Responses Received

Total Experience in Current Organization	Responses from Manufacturing Sector	Responses from Service Sector	Total No. of Responses	per cent of Total No. of Responses
Top management	12	21	33	18.23
Middle management	39	44	83	45.86
Operational management	22	43	65	35.91
Total	73	108	181	100

The managerial level-wise break-ups of the responses received for the questionnaire survey are given in Table 4.8. As per Table 4.8, 18.23 per cent responses are from top management, 45.86 per cent responses are from middle management and 35.91 per cent responses are from operational management. This is also right and acceptable because, the strategy formulation and related decisions are taken at senior management and implemented by middle management and operating management. Sustainability is an organization wide concept. The literature suggests that managers at all levels play important roles in varieties of organizational strategy (Floyd and Lane, 2000; Ireland, Hitt, and Vaidyanath, 2002).

In a generalized context, the role of top-level managers revolves around the making effective strategic decisions - decisions that are concerned with setting the firm's direction and reaching its objectives. The role of middle-level managers is to focus on effectively communicating information between the firm's two internal managerial levels (top-level managers and operating-level managers). The role of operating-level managers is to absorb relevant information gained from outside the firm while responding to middle-level managers' communication of information that is based on top-level managers' decisions (Floyd and Lane, 2000). As facilitators of information flow, middle-level managers help in sustainable actions (as determined by top-level executives) and their use in the form of competencies by first-level managers (Floyd and Lane, 2000; Ginsberg and Hay, 1994; Kanter, 1985). Pearce et al. (1997) and Floyd and Woolridge (1990, 1992, 1994), among others, recognized the role of middle managers in cultivating autonomous sustainable behavior and thereby fostering CE. King et al. (2001) proposed that because middle managers must reconcile top-level perspectives and lower-level implementation issues and they help to determine the use of competencies that affect firm performance. Using the competency characteristics of tacitness, robustness, embeddedness and consensus, King et al. (2001) found a strong link between middle-level managers' perceptions of these characteristics and firm performance. The ability of middle-level managers to champion the strategic alternatives emphasizes their role in enhancing adoption of sustainability practices.

Floyd and Lane (2000) identified first-level managers' roles within any strategic renewal as experimenting, adjusting, and conforming to the sub processes that are strategically developed at the upper levels. Sustainability is considered as a strategic renewal concept.

5.7   DATA PROCESSING AND THE UNIVARIATE ANALYSIS

In total, 281 respondents from 49 organizations have provided data for the questionnaire. First of all, the editing of the data was performed, where raw data was examined to detect errors and omissions in the responses. The reliability of respondents' response was tested as per the control questions introduced in various sections of the questionnaire. In case of three respondents, there was doubt regarding the reliability, as the reply to control questions was contradictory in nature. Therefore, these three responses were rejected. Some of the respondents did not respond to all sections/parts of the questionnaire, as they were requested to respond to a section only if they had actually experienced that particular situation during sustainability practice. Therefore, wherever the respondents have not replied to all questions for a particular section/part of the questionnaire, the response to the respective section(s) were rejected for the purpose of data analysis.

The data has been analyzed on computer using the 'Software Package for Social Sciences' (SPSS) Version 10.0. Univariate analysis of the data, for various strategy areas as identified earlier, is presented in the succeeding sections of this chapter.

4.7.1   Univariate Analysis of Macro Variables

Statistical description presented in Tables 5.10(a), (b) and (c) give the group statistics for organizational antecedents and sustainability strategy for total sample, manufacturing and services sectors respectively. There is little difference between the mean and median values of the macro variables, indicating that the distribution is close to the normal distribution and there is low effect of the extreme values of the variables. Further, the standard deviation values being low show that there is comparatively less spread around the mean.

Table 5.10(a): Group Statistics for Variables for Organizational Antecedents and Sustainability

	Mean	Median	Std. Deviation	Quart. Range
Green policy	5.2121	5.53276	0.16063	5.1-5.2
Green technology	4.6705	4.16763	0.35205	3.8-4.6
Green human sustainable resource	5.7576	5.25126	0.07576	3.1-5.7
Sustainability Strategy	5.4371	5.67219	0.36785	3.8-5.4

81

For the total sample, it is seen that organizations emphasize more on green policy, green technology, and green human sustainable resource for sustainability strategy. However, the organizations are also concerned with the sustainability strategy (mean=5.4).

Table 4.10(b): Group Statistics for Variables for Sustainability in relation to Manufacturing Sector

	Mean	Std. Deviation	Std. Error Mean
Green policy	4.2340	0.73326	0.32792
Green technology	4.3000	1.10609	0.49466
Production flexibility	5.2933	0.87223	0.39007
Sustainability Strategy	5.4271	0.62172	0.35895

In manufacturing sector, there is more emphasis on Green policy, Green technology and Production flexibility. This is also true since it is very important for the manufacturing organizations to have information about the current technology, market demand so that inventory costs can be reduced. Moreover, this will also help in achieving Just-in time delivery and reduce environmental emission. The study also shows that production flexibility is more important for reducing emission.

4.8 CONCLUDING REMARKS

The survey on drivers of sustainability strategy has been reported in this chapter. The detailed procedure followed for developing and validating the questionnaire is described, and univariate statistical analysis has been presented. The questionnaire contained ten dimensions, which were measured by 35 items. This questionnaire has undergone a rigorous validation process including the reliability tests. Its strategy have fully cleared the construct validity, and the results of mean values of the variables have been presented. Factors excluded in the factor analysis have been identified for more focused investigation during the extensive case studies of sustainability. Macro and micro variables getting high and low attention have been identified for further investigation during the case studies. The bivariate and multivariate analyses of the data collected through the survey are presented in the next chapter.

CHAPTER 5

VALIDATION OF CONCEPTUAL STRATEGY MODEL FOR SUSTAINABILITY*

5.1   INTRODUCTION

This chapter presents the bivariate and multivariate analysis of the data, in terms of correlation analysis and stepwise regression analysis, to test the hypotheses and to predict the relationships among the variables for evolving a sustainability model. The hypotheses have been identified on the basis of conceptual framework given in chapter three (Figure 3.1). The hypotheses have been evolved/formulated in terms of macro dimensions and also in terms of individual level micro dimensions. The macro dimensions relate to the directional thrusts, whereas the micro dimensions define the micro directional thrusts adopted by the organizations in implementing the macro dimensions during sustainable implementation.

The hypotheses formulated in chapter three are substantive or relational hypotheses (Kerlinher, 1973) in which conjectural statements of the relations between two or more variables are expressed. In the strict statistical sense, a substantive hypobook itself is not testable. It is tested against an alternative statement called null hypobook, which essentially means that there is no relation/influence with the second variable. First, the null hypobook is tested.

---

*Part of this chapter is published as:
Bhardwaj, B.R. (2012) Sustainability: A Case Study of HDFC Bank, chapter published in a book edited by Veena Panjwani and V. Sharma, Jagran Institute of Management, Kanpur.

If it is rejected, then it is assumed that the alternative hypobook is true. The level of significance in rejecting or accepting the hypotheses is also important. In testing of relational hypobook, generally the significance level of 5 per cent is taken, which means that the researcher is willing to take as much as 5 per cent risk of rejecting the null hypobook when it happens to be true (Kothari, 1985).

The bivariate analysis is used to determine and verify the degree of association among the variables, as stated in the particular hypobook. To determine the predictor relationships among the variables and develop sustainable model, the multivariate analysis (step-wise regression analysis) has been used.

The results of regression analysis, including the 'regression model summary' and the 'ANOVA analysis', are presented and discussed in detail for the first case. The full details are avoided in the later sections for the sake of brevity, where predictor variables are explained only on the basis of 'regression model summary'. However, full regressions results (including regression model summary and ANOVA analysis) for all the regression models are placed at Appendix-III.

5.2 TESTING HYPOTHESES OF ASSOCIATION FOR MACRO VARIABLES

The hypotheses of association compare and test the conceptual model framework where it is implied that sustainability outcome variable is dependent on internal environment. Starik and Rands (1995) examined the critical factors that influence the degree to which an organization's behaviors are ecologically sustainable, and behavioral and structural elements that are likely to be manifested by ecologically sustainable organizations (ESOs) were suggested.

5.2.1 Correlation Analysis

All eight macro variables of organizational antecedents and sustainability Outcome variable have been correlated using the Pearson correlation test for the full sample of 281 responses. The results obtained by the test are shown in Table 5.1. The statistical significance of correlation is indicated with single and double asterisks marks for probability levels of less than 0.05 and less than 0.01 respectively.

Table 5.1: Correlation of Macro Variables for the Total Sample

	GP	GHRM	GT	SO
GP	1			
GHRM	.367**	1		
GT	.454**	.557**	1	
SO	.501**	.566**	.683**	1

** Correlation is significant at the 0.01 level (2-tailed)

There is a significant correlation among the macro variables Green Policy (GT), Green human sustainable resource management (GHRM), Green technology (GT) and Sustainability Strategy (SO). The highest level of correlation is between Sustainability Strategy and Green technology (0.683) at 99 per cent confidence level. The explanation for that might be that in most of the organizations, desired Sustainability Strategy is not possible without proper adopting proper technology (Mangal, 2010; Bhardwaj, Bhatnagar, Gupta, 2012).

5.2.2 Regression Analysis

The hypotheses of association for macro variables are tested by regression analysis. Since all the relationships are established through correlation analysis, no variables are dropped while carrying out the regression analysis. The stepwise regression models are developed and tested for the five dependent macro variables, viz. Green policy, Green Human

Sustainable resource, Green Product flexibility, Green supply chain management and Green Technology.

Sustainability as Dependent Variable

The first major predictor of sustainability is Green policy (GP) as shown in Table 5.2 (a). The other predictors are Green Human Sustainable resource Development and Green Technology. All these variables together explain 54.2 per cent of the variance in CE; the rest is dependent on other variables and spurious variables not included in the model. The corresponding ANOVA values for the regression model are shown in Table 5.2 (b) indicating validation at 99 per cent confidence level. The coefficient summary as shown in Table 5.2 (c) gives Beta values of Green technology (GT), Green Human Sustainable resource (GHRM) and Green Product flexibility (GPF) as 0.459, 0.235 and 0.206 respectively, which are fairly representative of their impact on the Environmental Sustainability. Thus, Green policy (GP) is emerging as a major influence variable of Environmental Sustainability.

Table 5.2 (a): Regression Model Summary for Environmental Sustainability as Dependent Variable

Model	R	R Square	Adjusted R Square	Std. Error of the Estimate
1	.683	.466	.463	.90723
2	.719	.516	.511	.86619
3	.741	.549	.542	.83857

a Predictors: (Constant), GP
b Predictors: (Constant), GP, GHRM
c Predictors: (Constant), GP, GSCM, GPF
d Dependent Variable: SO

The model summary of macro variables for Sustainability strategy is given in Table 5.2 (d). Figure 5.1 shows the validated model for macro variables as predictors of Sustainability strategy.

Table 5.2 (b): ANOVA for Sustainability as Dependent Variable

Model		Sum of Squares	df	Mean Square	F	Sig.
1	Regression	128.763	1	128.763	156.442	.000
	Residual	147.330	179	.823		
	Total	276.093	180			
2	Regression	142.541	2	71.270	94.990	.000
	Residual	133.552	178	.750		
	Total	276.093	180			
3	Regression	151.626	3	50.542	71.874	.000
	Residual	124.466	177	.703		
	Total	276.093	180			

a Predictors: (Constant), GP
b Predictors: (Constant), GP, GHRM
c Predictors: (Constant), GP, GSCM, GPF
d Dependent Variable: SO

Table 5.2 (c): Coefficient Summary for Sustainability as Dependent Variable

Model		Unstandardized Coefficients		Standardized Coefficients	t	Sig.
		B	Std. Error	Beta		
1	(Constant)	1.441	.215		6.694	.000
	GP	.665	.053	.683	12.508	.000
2	(Constant)	.881	.244		3.619	.000
	GT	.519	.061	.533	8.495	.000
	WD	.306	.071	.269	4.285	.000
3	(Constant)	.504	.258		1.952	.053
	GHRM	.447	.063	.459	7.143	.000
	GPF	.267	.070	.235	3.818	.000
	GSCM	.220	.061	.206	3.594	.000

a Dependent Variable: SO

Table 5.2 (d): Model Summary of Macro Analysis of Sustainability as Dependent Variable

Dependent Variable	Independent Variables Entered in the Model	R Square	Hypotheses Accepted
SO	GP,GT,GHRM,GPF,GSCM	.549	H_{GP} , H_{GT} , H_{GPF}

The summary of the three regression models is shown in Table 5.2 (d) in terms of the independent variables acting as predictors, cumulative R square and the hypotheses codes (refer to section 3.4 for details) for the hypotheses accepted and the hypotheses rejected.

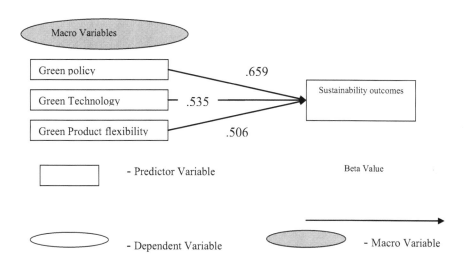

Figure 5.1: Validated Model for Macro Variables as Predictors of Sustainability

There are in all three hypotheses of association among macro variables and all of them have been accepted. The major predictors as per the hypotheses accepted relate to independent variables namely Green policy (GP), Green Human Sustainable resource Development (GHRM) and Green Technology (GT), which are either immediately preceding the dependent variables or at the best having a second level impact. The most critical among these variables is Green Product flexibility (GPF) which was not included in earlier studies.

Hence, the organizations intending to promote sustainability should have proper processes such as regular interdepartmental meetings to ensure the proper dispersion of environmental policy.

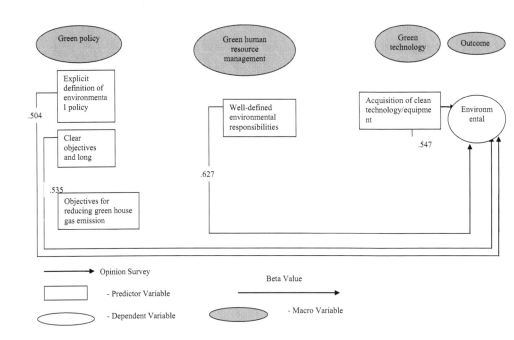

Figure 5.3: Validated Model of Micro Variables for Sustainability

This will help the organizations to reduce the environmental emission to meet sustainability parameters better. Moreover, without providing the autonomy and financial support to the employees for production, they will not be able to maintain the minimum level of output.

The coefficient of determination (R square) indicates that all these variables together explain variance in environmental sustainability. The regression coefficient 'Beta' shows the degree of association between these micro variables and New Business Creation. Here, the linear relationship is highly significant as the associated p-value is much less than 0.05.

Environmental sustainability as Dependent Variable

The macro variable analysis with the step-wise regression model has been concluded in three steps, as three macro variables namely green policy, green technology and green human sustainable resource management, production flexibility have entered the regression model (Table 5.5 (a)). This is explained as sustainability requires flexibility on the basis of customer information. Moreover, sustainability cannot be developed without providing autonomy to the employees. Hence, production flexibility has emerged as an important predictor of sustainability. The corresponding ANOVA values for the regression model and the coefficient summary are shown in Appendix III. The model summary of sustainability (macro variables) is given in Table 5.5 (b). Figure 5.4 shows the validated model for micro variables as predictors of Innovativeness.

Table 5.5 (a): Regression Model Summary for Sustainability as Dependent Variable (Macro Variables)

Model	R	R Square	Adjusted R Square	Std. Error of the Estimate
1	.742(a)	.551	.442	1.080

a   Predictors: (Constant), enhance water and energy conservation, environmental arguments in marketing, Explicit definition of environmental policy, emission filters and end-of-pipe control, acquisition of clean technology/equipment, reduces green house gas emission, green packaging, clear objectives and long term environmental plans

Micro Variables as Predictors of Sustainability

The stepwise regression analysis concluded in twelve steps (Table 5.5 (c)). There are several micro variables namely enhance water and energy conservation, environmental arguments in marketing, explicit definition of environmental policy, emission filters and end-of-pipe control, acquisition of clean technology/equipment, reduces green house gas emission, green packaging, clear objectives and long term environmental plans which have entered the regression analysis concluded in twelve steps.

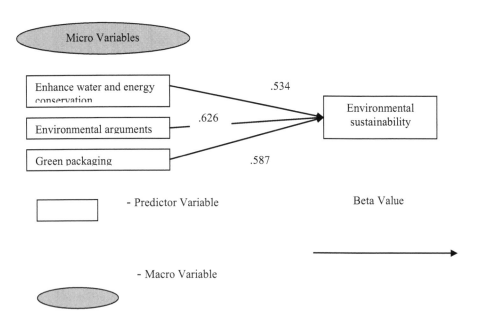

Figure 5.4: Validated Model for Macro Variables as Predictors of Sustainability

Each of these micro variables is hypothesized to be predictor of *Sustainability*. The regression analysis model summary shows that the micro variables namely explicit definition of environmental policy, emission filters and end-of-pipe control, acquisition of clean technology/equipment, reduces green house gas emission, green packaging, clear objectives and long term environmental plans are drivers of *Environmental Sustainability*.

Table 5.5(c): Model Summary of Green Human Sustainable resource Management and Environmental Sustainability

Mode l	R	R Square	Adjusted R Square	Std. Error of the Estimate
1	.681(a)	.464	.406	.867

a Predictors: (Constant), full-time employees devoted to environmental management, Explicit definition of environmental policy, well-defined environmental responsibilities, clear objectives and long term environmental plans

Table 5.5(c) describes the model summary of Green Human Sustainable resource Management and Environmental Sustainability. Each of these micro variables is hypothesized to be predictor of *Sustainability*. The regression analysis model summary shows that the micro variables namely full-time employees devoted to environmental management, explicit definition of environmental policy, well-defined environmental responsibilities, clear objectives and long term environmental plans are drivers of Environmental Sustainability.

Table 5.5(d): Model Summary of Green Policy and Green supply chain management

Model	R	R Square	Adjusted R Square	Std. Error of the Estimate
1	.426(a)	.181	.139	.865

a Predictors: (Constant), clear objectives and long term environmental plans, Explicit defination of environmental policy

Table 5.5(d) describes the model summary of Green Human Sustainable resource Management and Environmental Sustainability. Each of these micro variables is hypothesized to be predictor of *Sustainability*. The regression analysis model summary shows that the micro variables namely clear objectives and long term environmental plans, Explicit definition of environmental policy are drivers of Green supply chain management and enhances the suppliers to adopt green technology for least emission.

The details of the regression analysis in terms of ANOVA and coefficients are shown in Appendix III. The overall summary is given in Table 5.5 (d) and the validated model is shown in Figure 5.5.

5.3.3   Discussion on Hypotheses Testing

This section reports the summary of regression between organizational dimension, acting as independent variables, and the CE strategy, acting as dependent variables. The results reported in Tables 5.2 (d), show that among the most important predictors include clear objectives and long term environmental plans, explicit definition of environmental policy. This further validates the necessity of having proper explicit policy for enhancing green adoption and sustainable practices for dissemination of information at all levels.

Table 5.6: Syntheses of Learnings from Bivariate and Multivariate Analysis of *Sustainability*

Sustainability Dimensions	Dominant Macro Strategy	Dominant Micro Strategy
Environmental Sustainability	Environmental policy	Clear objectives and long term environmental plans, Explicit definition of environmental policy
	Green human sustainable resource practices	Full-time employees devoted to environmental management, natural environment training programmes for managers and employees
	Green supply chain management	Green packaging, preference for green products, recyclable or reusable packaging or container in logistics
	Green technology	Emission filters and end-of-pipe control, acquisition of clean technology/equipment

Sustainability Dimensions	Dominant Macro Strategy	Dominant Micro Strategy
Social	Green Product flexibility	Product flexibility, material flexibility
	Environmental policy	Clear objectives and long term environmental plans, Explicit definition of environmental policy

The positive nature of the relationship points out the fact that the employees should be given the autonomy in terms of abilities and selection of business ideas to motivate CE. Also, it is important to have management support in terms of financial support for CE concept.

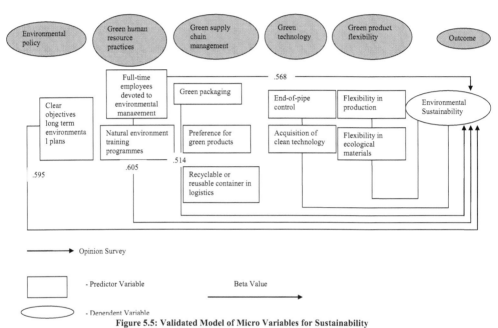

Environmental
policy

Green human
resource
practices

Green supply
chain
management

Green
technology

Green product
flexibility

Outcome

.568

Full-time
employees
devoted to
environmental
management

Green packaging

End-of-pipe
control

Flexibility in
production

Environmental
Sustainability

Clear
objectives
long term
environmenta
l plans

Natural environment
training
programmes

Preference for
green products

Acquisition of
clean technology

Flexibility in
ecological
materials

.595

.605

.514

Recyclable or
reusable container in
logistics

———▶ Opinion Survey

☐ - Predictor Variable   Beta Value ——————▶

⬭ - Dependent Variable

Figure 5.5: Validated Model of Micro Variables for Sustainability

96

5.4 CONCLUDING REMARKS

The questionnaire survey data has been analyzed through correlation technique and regression analysis to test the macro as well as micro hypotheses evolved for the study. Hypotheses testing are based on the strength of correlation among the variables. Regression analysis gives useful results regarding model formulation. The results of the study have been presented and discussed in this chapter. The key issues and dominant/useful organization level practices have been identified. These results also provide useful deep-insight into the antecedents of sustainability.

CHAPTER 6

CASE STUDIES OF SUSTAINABILITY PRACTICES IN SELECT ORGANIZATIONS

6.1   INTRODUCTION

The increasing importance of sustainable behavior in business has enhanced its impact on supply chain management. Firms foster sustainability in their supplier base in reaction to growing sustainability requirements in various ways, including sustainable supplier co-operation. Knowledge about the effects of sustainable supplier co-operation on firm performance is limited; therefore, this study tests antecedents and implications of sustainable supplier co-operation according to the triple bottom line. A survey of Western European firms reveals that sustainable supplier co-operation has generally positive effects on firm performance across social, green and economic dimensions. However, only green practices have positive significant effects on economic performance, not social practices (e.g., child labour rules). In contrast to practitioner perceptions, investments in sustainability, for example through sustainable supplier co-operation does indeed result in sufficient returns.

This chapter examines the key internal organizational factors through case study method. The focus is on understanding the internal organizational factors promoting or stifling sustainability efforts.

*Part of this chapter has been published as:

Bhardwaj, B.R. (2012) Book Review on Cases in Management, edited by Dr. Venkat Subhramanium, Dr. Sachin S. Vernekar, Ms Preety Wadhwa, BVIMR, Management Edge, Vol. 5, No. 2, ISSN No. 0976-0431.

The main objective of this study is to assess the organizational level practices, identified earlier in chapters two and three, with reference to the contextual parameter including internal organizational factor's zone of influence and set the stage for better environment to enhance sustainable concept.

This study has been taken up to understand the micro issues related to organizational antecedents emerging from the pilot study and questionnaire survey study. Moreover, the case studies are aimed to understand the various sustainability initiatives within the organizations and the processes to sustain it. These case studies also highlight the actions taken by these organizations the performances thereof.

6.2   METHODOLOGY FOR THE CASE STUDY

Keeping in view the objectives and scope of the overall study, the case studies in this chapter are devoted to sustainability practices.

The study adopts dual case study approach where unit of analysis are (a) firm level (its internal environment components) (b) product/service level (Yin, 1994). Data was gathered through observations, literature available and questionnaire based interviews. The questionnaire measured responses on a scale of 1-6, 1 being "strongly disagree" and 6 being "strongly agree". The interview notes were prepared according to '24-hours rule' (Yin, 1994; 2002). According to this rule, detailed interview notes and impressions collected need to be cross checked immediately within one day of the interview.

The two organizations and their practices were selected on the basis of purposive sampling. These organizations are: Mahindra and Mahindra and ABB.

Mahindra and Mahindra is a company primarily dealing with manufacturing of auto cars. ABB is involved into electrical equipments manufacturing.

The case studies have been prepared by conducting interviews and the study of detailed reports present in the organization. However, the historic data regarding the organization has been collected from company records and company websites ans sustainability reports. Structured interviews of the managers/executives were held during personal visits by the researcher to the company design offices and manufacturing facilities.

The managerial practices that affect sustainability fall into five general categories, namely, challenge, freedom, sustainable resources, work-group features, supervisory encouragement, and organizational support. To find out the links between work environment and sustainability, we have used three methodologies: experiments, interviews, and surveys. While controlled experiments allowed us to identify causal links, the interviews and surveys gave us insight into the richness and complexity of innovation within business organizations. We have studied two organizations and within these 95 individuals and many teams. In each research initiative, our goal has been to identify which managerial practices, processes and systems are linked to sustainability strategy and which are not. For instance, in our research, we interviewed employees from these organizations and asked them to describe in detail the sustainability events or initiatives in their organizations. In my research, I was given access to personnel involved with those ventures, including the documents about these ventures. From 2003 to 2006, I conducted more than 105 interviews and sifted through hundreds of documents. We then closely studied these transcripts of interviews, noting the managerial practices which created the environment – or other patterns that appeared repeatedly in the successful innovative event and, conversely, in those that were unsuccessful. Our research has also been bolstered by a quantitative survey instrument developed through pilot study. Taken by employee at top, middle, and bottom level of an organization, the questionnaire consists of 35 questions used to assess the internal environment of the organization, such as management support for sustainability efforts.

7.2.1 7S Framework

The 7S Framework first appeared in "The Art of Japanese Management" by Richard Pascale and Anthony Athos in 1981. They had been looking at how Japanese sector had been so successful, at around the same time that Tom Peters and Robert Waterman were exploring what made a company excellent. The 7S model was born at a meeting of the four authors in 1978. It went on to appear in "In Search of Excellence" by Peters and Waterman, and was taken up as a basic tool by the global management consultancy McKinsey: it's sometimes known as the McKinsey 7S model. Managers, they said, need to take account of all seven of the factors to be sure of successful implementation of a strategy - large or small. They're all interdependent, so if one fails to pay proper attention to one of them, it can bring the others crashing down around you. The relative importance of each factor varies over time. The 3Ss across the top of the model are described as 'Hard Ss':

Strategy: The direction and scope of the company over the long term.

Structure: The basic organization of the company, its departments, reporting lines, areas of expertise, and responsibility (and how they inter-relate).

Systems: Formal and informal procedures that govern everyday activity, covering everything from management information systems, through to the systems at the point of contact with the customer (retail systems, call centre systems, online systems, etc.).

The 4Ss across the bottom of the model are less tangible, more cultural in nature, and were termed 'Soft Ss' by McKinsey:

Skills: The sustainable capabilities and competencies that exist within the company. What it does best.

Shared values: The values and beliefs of the company. Ultimately they guide employees towards 'valued' behavior.

Staff: The company's people sustainable resources and how they are developed, trained, and motivated.

Style: The leadership approach of top management and the company's overall operating approach.

7.2.2 The Sustainable SAP-LAP Framework

The cases have been analyzed using 7S framework and flexible system methodology based on the SAP-LAP (Situation-Actor-Process, Learning-Action-Performance) framework (Sushil, 1993, 1994, 1997, 1999, 2000) to evolve the 'learning issues' regarding the actual practices and to bring out the 'suggested actions' for 'improvement in the performance'. The methodology is applied in two steps comprising of SAP analysis and LAP synthesis. In SAP analysis, the case is described through three components that define the sustainable interplay of reality. These components are situation, actors and processes. These are definable within a context and interact flexibly on multiple planes in the ambiguous reality. Situation is the present status covering the environment, business opportunity, including technological potential and sustainability practices undertaken by the organizations. The participants, including the managers, sustainability champion/team leader (s) who influence the situation and alter it by their actions or inaction are termed as actors. The procedural steps, including sustainability concept, taken by the actors who alter the situation are termed as the process. Some aspects of the process may be explicitly definable while some others would be implicit. Any sustainable behavior that alters the situation has the potential of being a process or a part of a process. The SAP matrix is formed on the basis of the internal and external actors for the organization. The internal actors include the employees of the organization; whereas the external actors include the external partners and suppliers. SAP matrix explains the two situations in terms of before and after the implementation of the sustainability initiatives within the organization.

SAP analysis leads to the second phase, which is called LAP synthesis, having three components i.e., learning issues, actions and performance. Learning issues emphasize the typicality of the situation as well as some features of the uniqueness. In the context of sustainability approach, it covers the outcome of the practices, policies and the product developing and idea generation concept and also the reasons thereof. Learning issues also lead to action, which when taken would lead to improved performance. This should result in high level of sustainability strategy for the organizations.

In each case study, prevalent situation in the context of sustainability practices have been identified. The current environment scenario covering the business opportunities/challenges, customers, competitors, suppliers/venders have been discussed. The roles played by all actors have also been described. The process part deals with management practices and developmental concept towards sustainability practices to meet the desired organizational goals and objectives, keeping in view the issues mentioned earlier.

The sustainable SAP-LAP framework was used to understand the external and internal environmental changes with respect to time (five years taken for analysis) (Sushil, 2000a). Sustainable SAP analysis gives the analysis of Situation, Actors, and Processes with respect to time. This Sustainable SAP analysis is with reference to internal and external environment helps to understand the situation after and before CE initiatives were taken up.

6.3   CASE STUDY I: SUSTAINABILITY PRACTICES AT ABB

ABB has launched its annual Sustainability report highlighting a new strategy and the progress made in 2011 in embedding sustainability values and considerations in business processes. "We can see year-on-year the way in which health and safety, and environmental, social and security issues are becoming part of our business case and success," said Adam Roscoe, head of Sustainability Affairs. "Our new sustainability strategy is part of that process and will help us capture the benefits of a sustainable

approach to business." Among the highlights was the finalization of the new strategy –
known as Sustainability Strategy 2015+ - after an analysis of the widest-ever
consultation process with internal and external stakeholders. The new strategy, formally
being launched in 2012, was produced in alignment with the ABB Group strategy
review.

ABB's sustainability strategy

The sustainability strategy is based on five focus areas – all of them part of or directly
related to ABB business operations – and establishes a governance board for the first
time. The ABB Sustainability Board will comprise the entire Executive Committee; it
will oversee how sustainability policies and programs support business goals and
aspirations, and monitor progress. The new strategy is being supported by the
development of key performance indicators to measure progress, a competence
management and organizational development program, and additional measures to
communicate with stakeholders. On environmental issues, the 2011 Sustainability
report highlights innovative products and systems, the progress on reducing energy
consumption within the Group, the phasing out of hazardous substances, and efforts to
reduce ABB's carbon footprint in areas such as manufacturing, logistics and
transportation.

Green human sustainable resource management

The value of training in raising ABB's performance and standards is also featured.
Health and safety training helped ABB to a year in which there were no fatalities in

operations for the first time in a decade; security and crisis management sessions helped the company ensure the safety of employees and subcontractors, as well as business continuity, in times of crisis - most notably following the Fukushima tragedy in Japan and the political upheavals in the Middle East and North Africa; and training on supply chain and human rights are also contributing to greater awareness of the kinds of issues ABB faces and helping the company towards better risk management. "One of the core messages that emerges from the report is the way in which sustainability issues are increasingly being embedded in business processes – particularly project risk review, supply chain and our mergers and acquisitions process," said Roscoe.

"ABB's corporate tagline is 'Power and Productivity for the better world' and we want to deliver on that promise to contribute to 'a better world' – a more sustainable society in which a growing population has fair access to sustainable resources, health and well-being now and into the future."

The Sustainability report also reviews how ABB performed against the targets it set for the two years until the end of 2011. One of the key statistics is that ABB was able to reduce its energy use by 5.5 percent in those two years – slightly above the target that was set.

- Training: Security and Crisis Management training / exercises in all regions during 2012 as part of regular three year program; Human Rights training for senior employees in 12 main manufacturing/export countries/regions by end of 2012

- Management systems: Implement security and crisis management systems and programs across all regions, according to priorities based on risks and needs

- Consolidate implementation of programs identified in existing EC approved OHS Plan: Maintain strategic, Group-led OHS programs, such as OHS leadership training

- Maintain and increase the reach of BU-specific OHS initiatives - Ensure implementation of country strategic OHS plans, with quarterly KPI reporting

Sustainability performance

As every year, ABB reports against the Global Reporting Initiative Indicators, the internationally-recognized standard for sustainability reporting. Credibility is further enhanced by the assurance provided by an external company, Det Norske Veritas, which examined the environmental and social data in the report.

For ABB, sustainability is about balancing economic success, environmental stewardship and social progress to benefit all our stakeholders.

Sustainability considerations cover how the company designs and manufactures products, what it offers to customers, how they engage suppliers, how they assess risks and opportunities, and how they behave in the communities where they operate and towards one another, while striving to ensure the health, safety and security of employees, contractors and others affected by its concept.

Green technology

ABB's products, systems, solutions and services are designed to improve our customers' businesses - centered on improving grid reliability and increasing industrial productivity - while lowering environmental impact.

The company seeks to minimize the environmental impact of our technologies and products, passing on this expertise to customers and suppliers, at the same time as trying to ensure that our manufacturing processes are environmentally friendly and energy-efficient.

Green product flexibility

In the operations, ABB strives to reduce the use of energy and materials, streamline the means of transporting goods, reduce the impact of business travel, phase out hazardous materials, design eco-efficient and recyclable products, and enhance suppliers' performance. Much can be achieved through sharing best practice. Water-borne paint systems developed at one factory, for example, have been introduced at similar sites worldwide to reduce emissions of organic solvents.

Improving performance also includes the design phase of new products and processes. Design engineers receive training and tools to carry out Life Cycle Assessments to evaluate a product's environmental impact throughout its life cycle. Four hundred sustainability officers, many of them based at our factories, implement Group and national objectives at ABB's approximately 360 sites and offices worldwide. They ensure that all manufacturing facilities comply with ISO 14001 and OHSAS 18001 international standards on the management of environmental and health and safety risks. Close collaboration with external sustainability organizations and universities also helps ABB to establish effective programs to support its improvement initiatives.

ABB Sustainability and Ethical Principles

ABB seeks to uphold the highest standards in business ethics and integrity, including supporting efforts of national and international authorities to establish and enforce high integrity standards for all businesses. ABB has a Code of Conduct and a Supplier Code of Conduct in place to help achieve these standards, and seeks continuous improvement in its ethical, environmental, social and human rights performance. ABB seeks to integrate health and safety into all concept, encourage safety leadership at every level and ensure appropriate sustainable resources to achieve performance. ABB is committed to develop sustainable resource-efficient products and systems, to reduce the impacts of its own operations, and to engage in an ongoing dialogue with customers to help them select the most environmentally sound products, systems and solutions.

ABB's Human Rights and Social Policies draw on the Universal Declaration of Human Rights, the ILO Core Conventions on Labor Standards, UN Global Compact, the OECD Guidelines for Multinational Enterprises and the Social Accountability 8000 standard. The ABB Human Rights and Social Policies specifically reference ILO Core Conventions as the minimum to be achieved, with respect to non-discrimination, prohibition of child and enforced labor, freedom of association and the right to engage in collective bargaining.

Green supply chain management

ABB seeks to do business with suppliers which have implemented governance, integrity, environmental, social, health and safety and human rights standards, as reflected in the ABB Supplier Code of Conduct. ABB strives to create a secure working environment for its employees, contractors and third parties. The company equally seeks to maintain adequate management systems to minimize impact on people, assets and reputation, should an incident occur.

Social Sustainability Strategy

Through our business, ABB contributes to a more sustainable society - "a better world" – one in which a growing population has fair access to sustainable resources, health and well-being now and into the future. They do this by engaging customers, employees, suppliers, business partners and communities to create innovative solutions to some of the world's challenges. These include the need to strengthen sustainable resource efficiency - how to do more with less for a more sustainable world. Embedding processes within ABB's daily business practice which support these goals is key to success, both for the company and our stakeholders.

Goal

By 2015 and beyond, ABB will be a leading contributor to a more sustainable world and will be recognized as a top-performing company in terms of sustainable business practice.

Green policy

They work to ensure that sustainability considerations and values are understood, implemented, measured and communicated across ABB's value chain, so they become a seamless part of business practice and help our customers to be more effective and successful. In short, to work in the knowledge that sustainability is good for our business, for our customers and for society.

Sustainability Objectives 2012

One of the key elements to implement the Sustainability Strategy 2015+ is the development of business-relevant KPIs and objectives, in consultation with the businesses and functions. This process is under way, with the aim to develop the next full set of ABB Sustainability Objectives by Q3 2012.

For 2012 only, they have decided to continue and adapt the Sustainability Objectives 2010 - 2011, to allow adequate time to consult and to develop and test the next full set of objectives. The 2012 objectives are consistent with on-going programs and also take account of those objectives from 2010 - 2011 that have been achieved.

The Sustainability Objectives 2012 are intended to sustain and further improve:

- ABB's environmental performance
- a safe, secure and responsible working environment
- sustainability performance in the supply chain.

The objectives are as follows:

- **Sustainable resource efficiency:** Energy: All sites to reduce use of energy by 2.5% annually. Water: Action plans at facilities in water stressed regions

- Travel: Develop action plans to reduce the environmental impact of business air travel

- Formal review of social, security, OHS and environmental risks instituted at early stage of divisional project risk assessments

- Maintain & improve crisis management, security and human rights capability

Sustainability focus areas

ABB's customers and stakeholders expect us to consider long-term sustainability aspects over the entire value chain. The key focus areas – those that are material to ABB - are:

- Developing world-class products, systems and services to lower our customers' energy use, reduce their emissions and improve sustainable resource efficiency on a long-term basis.

- Ensuring the operations are energy and sustainable resource efficient.

- Proactively ensuring our suppliers, employees and business partners work in a safe, healthy and secure environment, and to the highest standards of integrity.

- Creating value and promoting social development in communities where we operate.

- Strengthening employees' involvement and commitment to improve the company's sustainability performance.

112

- Improve sustainability performance in the supply chain through the Supplier Sustainability Development Program:

  - 110 audits in high-risk countries in 2012

  - Face-to-face training with 250 suppliers in defined, high-risk countries
  - On-line training developed and available

Corporate responsibility: Seeking higher standards

ABB is committed to maintaining high social, environmental, human rights, ethical and governance standards for the benefit of all stakeholders. Corporate responsibility reflects the company's values and behavior to its stakeholders.

The company has several policies and standards in place to underpin those core values, covering business ethics and governance, the Code of Conduct, and policies such as the Group Social and Human Rights policies. These are all supported by internal Group directives and instructions.

There are many stakeholders impacted by ABB policies and performance, ranging from employees and subcontractors to customers, suppliers and communities where ABB has operations. The company recognizes the importance of wide-ranging stakeholder engagement to help it achieve best practice and sustainable benefit for stakeholders. Sustainability experts within the company also work with business divisions and other group functions to raise awareness of potential risk and improve performance.

One of the core areas of corporate responsibility is human rights. ABB is seeking to raise its standards, and increase its understanding and mitigation of human rights risk. A Human Rights policy and public statement were approved in 2007, complementing existing policies for raising social, environmental, health and safety and business ethics performance.

Social policy

ABB's social policy was adopted in February 2001. It draws on five sources: the United Nations' Universal Declaration of Human Rights, the International Labor Organization's fundamental principles on rights at work, the OECD Guidelines for Multinational Enterprises, the Global Sullivan Principles and the Social Accountability 8000 (SA 8000) standard, an auditable standard for the protection of workers' rights developed by the Council on Economic Priorities Accreditation Agency.

We engage in stakeholder review and consultations on this policy to ensure that it is continuously improved. Our policy aims:

1. ABB in society

To contribute within the scope of our sustainable capabilities to improving economic, environmental and social conditions through open dialogue with stakeholders and through active participation in common efforts.

2. Human rights

To support and respect the protection of internationally proclaimed human rights. Employees and contractors engaged as security personnel shall observe international human rights norms in their work.

3. Children and young workers

To ensure that minors are properly protected; and as a fundamental principle, not to employ children or support the use of child labor, except as part of government-approved youth training schemes (such as work-experience programs).

4. Freedom of engagement

To require that all employees enter into employment with the company of their own free will; and not to apply any coercion when engaging employees or support any form of forced or compulsory labor.

5. Health and safety

To provide a safe and healthy working environment at all sites and facilities and to take adequate steps to prevent accidents and injury to health arising out of the course of work by minimizing, so far as is reasonably practicable, the causes of hazards inherent in the working environment.

6. Employee consultation and communication

To facilitate regular consultation with all employees to address areas of concern. To respect the right of all personnel to form and join trade unions of their choice and to bargain collectively. To ensure that representatives of personnel are not the subject of discrimination and that such representative have access to their members in the workplace. To make sure, in any case of major layoffs, that a social benefits and guidance plan is in place, and already known to employees or their official representatives.

7. Equality of opportunity

To offer equality of opportunity to all employees and not to engage in or support discrimination in hiring, compensation, access to training, promotion, termination or retirement based on ethnic and national origin, caste, religion, disability, sex, age, sexual orientation, union membership, or political affiliation.

8. Harassment and disciplinary practices

To counteract the use of mental or physical coercion, verbal abuse or corporal/hard-labor punishment; and not to allow behavior, including gestures, language and physical contact, that is sexual, coercive, threatening, abusive or exploitative. To develop and maintain equitable procedures to deal with employee grievances and disciplinary practices.

9. Working hours

To comply with applicable laws and industry standards on working hours, including over-time.

10. Compensation

To ensure that wages paid meet or exceed the legal or industry minimum standards and are always sufficient to meet basic needs of personnel and to provide some discretionary income. To ensure that wage and benefits composition are detailed clearly and regularly for workers, and that compensation is rendered in full compliance with all applicable laws and in a manner convenient to workers. To ensure that labor-only contracting arrangements and false apprenticeship schemes are not used to avoid fulfilling ABB's obligations under applicable laws pertaining to labor and social security legislation and regulations.

11. Suppliers

To establish and maintain appropriate procedures to evaluate and select major suppliers and subcontractors on their ability to meet the requirements of ABB's social policy and principles and to maintain reasonable evidence that these requirements are continuing to be met.

12. Community involvement

To promote and participate in community engagement concept that actively foster economic, environmental, social and educational development, as part of ABB's commitment to the communities where it operates.

13. Business ethics

To uphold the highest standards in business ethics and integrity and to support efforts of national and international authorities to establish and enforce high ethical standards for all businesses.

Human Rights policy and statement

ABB is committed to developing an organizational culture which implements a policy of support for internationally recognized human rights and seeks to avoid complicity in human rights abuses. We support the principles contained within the Universal

Declaration of Human Rights, the OECD Guidelines for Multinational Enterprises and the ILO Core Conventions on Labour Standards.

ABB seeks to identify, assess and manage human rights impacts within our spheres of influence and concept in line with the following policy aims:

1. Employees

To respect the human rights of our employees as established in the ILO's Declaration on Fundamental Principles and Rights at Work, including non-discrimination, prohibition of child and enforced labor, and freedom of association and the right to engage in collective bargaining.

2. Suppliers and Contractors

To establish and maintain appropriate procedures to evaluate and select major suppliers and contractors, based on ABB's human rights and social policies, and to monitor their performance where appropriate. To advance the application of the ILO Declaration on Fundamental Principles and Rights at Work through engagement and collaboration where necessary.

3. Local Communities

To respect the cultures, customs and values of the people in communities in which we operate.

To contribute, within the scope of our sustainable capabilities, to promote the fulfillment of human rights through improving economic, environmental and social conditions and serve as a positive influence in communities in which we operate.

To seek to have open dialogue with stakeholders and participate in community engagement concept.

To aim to ensure the provision of security is consistent with international standards of best practice and the laws of the countries in which we operate, using security services only where necessary and requiring the use of force only when necessary and proportionate to the threat.

4. Society

To participate where appropriate in public affairs in a non-partisan and responsible way to promote internationally recognized human rights.

To seek to play a positive role, within our spheres of influence, in capacity-building for the realization of human rights within countries of operation.

To promote the realization of environmental sustainability and development through our core business and through our participation in other multistakeholder concept where appropriate.

To uphold the highest standards in business ethics and integrity and where appropriate to support efforts of national and international authorities to establish and enforce high ethical standards for all businesses.

ABB Human Rights statement

ABB is committed to developing an organizational culture which implements a policy of support for the internationally recognized human rights contained within the Universal Declaration of Human Rights and seeks to avoid complicity in human rights abuses.

Their commitment to the realization of human rights is embedded in the Group's human rights and social policies and the criteria appropriate to ABB in the Global Reporting Initiative. Human rights are part of our non-financial risk assessment of operations. ABB is involved in multilateral efforts to support human rights such as the United Nations Global Compact and Business Leaders Initiative on Human Rights.

Human rights performance information

Human rights performance: Other GRI indicators

HR1 Significant investment agreements that include human rights

ABB maintains and regularly reviews a list of sensitive countries where it has, or considers engaging in, business operations. Human rights, as well as legal, financial and security criteria, are included in risk assessments, and are among the factors in deciding whether ABB does business in a particular country. Based partly or wholly on human rights considerations, ABB has not taken any business with Myanmar or North Korea for several years. ABB completed its withdrawal from Sudan in June 2009.

HR4 Non-discrimination violations

All countries in ABB's sustainability management program are asked to report any incidents of discrimination. Five substantiated cases of discrimination and 32 of harassment were reported in 2011, resulting in six terminations, three resignations and a range of other measures, including warnings, counseling and further training.

HR5, HR6, HR7 Operations at risk

Freedom of association and collective bargaining, child labor, forced or compulsory labor. There were no ABB operations identified during 2011 to be at significant risk concerning employee rights to freedom of association and collective bargaining, incidents of child labor, or incidents of forced or compulsory labor. In ABB's supply chain, 11 cases of underage labor were found at two suppliers in 2011. Immediate corrective measures were introduced to safeguard the rights of the children.

HR8 Training of security personnel in human rights

ABB sees the training of security personnel, as well as ABB country and regional managers, on the human rights dimensions of security work as important. It has been part of general security training in different parts of the world for several years. By the end of 2011 more than 850 managers in more than 90 percent of ABB countries had been trained on crisis management; depending on local needs, some of those training contained sessions on human rights.

New Group-wide security guidelines are being drawn up, based on the Voluntary Principles for Security and Human Rights. They are due to be finalized in 2012. ABB already requires due diligence on all security companies according to ABB and international standards, and the new guidelines will establish standard operating procedures for security providers to include instructions on human rights issues.

In addition, ABB's country and regional security heads have been made aware of growing stakeholder expectations that human rights need to be observed, and of the kinds of human rights issues that could arise in communities where ABB has operations or business concept.

HR9 Indigenous rights violations

All countries in ABB's sustainability management program are asked to report any incidents of indigenous rights violations. No such incidents were reported in 2011.

HR10 Percentage of total number of operations that have been subject to human rights reviews and/or impact assessments

These data are not available. ABB is involved as a supplier in thousands of projects worldwide each year. Depending on the scope and size of the project – such as larger power infrastructure projects – some will require at least an Environmental and Social Impact Assessment performed by the customer. The data are currently not consolidated by ABB.

HR11 Number of grievances related to human rights filed, addressed and resolved through formal grievance mechanism.

ABB has a number of formal grievance mechanisms, including a third-party run Business Ethics hotline available round the clock and an Ombuds program, where employees can report concerns confidentially. Figures are available for cases of discrimination and harassment (HR 4); other data are not available.

Sustainability in the supply chain: Developing strength in the networks

ABB's suppliers – from raw materials to subcontractors – are an extension of our own business. As we pursue our growth strategy to 2015, strong supplier performance ensuring resilient, cost-effective and sustainable supply chains will be a key factor in our success.

When qualifying suppliers, ABB has long considered sustainability principles alongside the more traditional aspects of quality, cost and on-time delivery. They require suppliers to identify the health and safety and environmental risks in the scope of their supply to us, and we request evidence of social and human rights policies, and sustainability improvement programs. On-site audits have been conducted by ABB personnel and by the suppliers themselves in a self-assessment process.

The ABB Supplier Code of Conduct (SCC) defines the minimum standards for any company wishing to sell to ABB. All suppliers are required to fulfill their contracts according to standards comparable with those defined in the SCC. The code covers supplier performance in fair and legal labor conditions, occupational health and safety, environmental responsibility and business ethics. The SCC also requires suppliers to be responsible for the sustainability performance of the sub-suppliers they hire to provide direct or indirect goods or services to ABB.

To embed these principles both in our supply base and within our own supply chain management network, we are continuing our Supplier Sustainability Development Program. Commenced in late 2009, the program aims to develop suppliers into strategic business partners who share our commitment to sustainability and to build capacity in our supply chain management to ensure appropriate support for improving supplier performance.

The program began with a series of pilot sustainability audits of ABB suppliers conducted by a third-party company in 2009 and 2010. The audits focused on suppliers in higher risk countries, producing commodities using hazardous processes, such as castings and forgings, and were used to road-test new, Group-wide guidelines for auditors.

During 2011, we began full implementation of the program, conducting 125 third-party audits in 18 countries, with two-thirds of those audits in "high risk" countries, such as emerging economies. These audits revealed a number of situations where ABB's standards were not met. The issues which were discovered included excessive overtime, poor waste disposal practices, or a lack of appropriate protective equipment for workers. In particular, at two suppliers 11 cases of child labor were detected. As soon as these cases were detected, the children were accompanied home by supplier personnel. The suppliers committed to pay for the children's education and to continue to pay the children's wages until they reached majority age, at which time the children would be allowed to recommence work at the supplier's premises.

ABB supply chain or quality managers are assigned to follow up the corrective action plans developed by the suppliers following their audits. Suppliers can be re-audited to ensure closure of corrective actions. Should a supplier not comply with their corrective action commitments, ABB aims to commence a process to de-source that supplier. To date, they have not de-sourced any suppliers as a result of sustainability audit findings.

Audits conducted during 2011 targeted both "high risk" and developed countries, to test our assumption that the majority of high risk findings would occur in high risk countries. The assumptions were confirmed, and in 2012 they will focus the sustainability audit program in China, India, Mexico, Brazil and Eastern Europe, aiming to conduct 110 third-party audits during the period.

They developed and delivered supplier awareness training to over 200 suppliers in India and China in face-to-face sessions in 2011 to help them better understand our Supplier Code of Conduct and to help them to evaluate and improve their sustainability performance. In 2012, they will continue to expand the capacity-building program, conducting more face-to-face training with suppliers, developing online training modules and delivering specific training for our own supply chain staff, embedding that training in the existing Supply Chain Excellence program.

In addition to the focused Supplier Sustainability Development Program, ABB's global sustainability network also conducts focused environmental audits of suppliers, as part of our own facilities' ISO 14001 management systems. More than 950 documented environmental audits of suppliers were performed during 2011. Overall, more than 50 percent of approximately 1,500 key suppliers are externally certified to ISO 14001 and a further 10 percent have implemented "selfdeclared" environmental management systems.

The results show that they still have work to do to embed sustainability principles along our supply chain. We are committed to building capacity both within their own organization and supply base, and believe that improved sustainability performance of our suppliers is a prerequisite for ABB's growth and improved performance into the future.

Working in the community: Committed to the community

ABB engages in the community because they believe it is the right thing to do and know it is good for our business if they are welcome in the areas where they operate. From supporting schools in Brazil, India and South Africa, to charity fund-raisers in North America, or helping athletes at European Special Olympics, to an anti-desertification program in China, we work in a wide variety of ways to strengthen environmental, social and economic development in the communities close to their sites and offices.

ABB's community engagement focuses on two core areas: education and health care. In total, ABB employees and companies donated approximately $6.5 million in funding and provided about 4,000 man-days in volunteering time in 2011 – a sharp increase in the number contributed in 2010. For ABB, community engagement goes beyond philanthropy. The company needs local "buy-in" from communities close to our operations; it's essential to our social license to operate. Support for education projects not only raises standards but in some cases helps ABB to recruit qualified engineers and other staff.

They support schools, students and universities in different ways. There are schemes in countries such as Brazil, Czech Republic, Chile, China, India, Peru, Poland and South

Africa to help young people and schools in disadvantaged areas. In China, for example, we support students through involvement in a scholarship scheme called the New Great Wall project.

There is clear business value in some of the programs. In Finland, for example, the company contributed to four universities in 2011 as a way of ensuring that engineering graduates have the qualities required by the industry. In Saudi Arabia, ABB holds annual training programs for students from vocational institutes and offers technical training to engineering students.

In other countries, support for universities is extended to individual student projects. In Finland, the company backed students developing solar technology for a sailing boat, while in Turkey, ABB supported a series of innovative projects at different universities. Elsewhere, such as in Chile and Peru, contributions are made towards building or improving school facilities.

ABB employees enjoy volunteering for projects. The largest such effort in 2011, which was backed by 1,000 man-days, was in the India, Middle East and Africa region. About 5,000 ABB employees and subcontractors – as well as family members – took part in a week of concept to promote greater health and safety awareness and performance in the workplace, at home and on the roads.

During the week, a series of training sessions and fun events were held in all Gulf Arab states, as well Egypt, Jordan, India and parts of Africa. The events included road safety awareness sessions, safety inspections of employees' vehicles, safety observation tours by management and special trainings for working at height and electrical safety, as well as quizzes, a photo competition, health checks and relaxation therapy for employees.

In recognition, ABB won the Middle East Electricity Corporate Social Responsibility Award of the Year for our work to continually improve our health and safety standards.

The second largest volunteering effort in 2011 was in Germany where about 100 employees used a week of their holidays to support athletes with intellectual disabilities at the Special Olympics. More than 2,000 ABB employees have supported this annual event since the company began its involvement a decade ago. Similar events are backed by ABB volunteers in Italy, the United Kingdom and the United States.

The company is also involved in a range of projects focusing on health care. Employees in Canada and the United States raise funds through donations and charity events for hospitals and health-care organizations. In South Africa, we support a project to help orphans of HIV/Aids victims; in Egypt, the company helps a leading pediatric hospital in Cairo; and in the United Kingdom fund-raising efforts are focused on a cancer care charity.

ABB does not have a Group-wide method of measuring the impacts of community projects, but this is under development. For the time being, individual countries have their own ways of measuring success.

- ABB in Switzerland has an innovative program to give a second chance of an apprenticeship to young people who failed to complete their first apprenticeship. Success is defined as completion of their "second chance" and/or finding a job. More than 60 young people have taken part in the scheme so far with an 80 percent success rate.

- In India, the success of ABB's support for six government schools in communities where we operate is measured and evaluated. The results include 1,670 children from disadvantaged backgrounds who received a free midday meal paid by ABB employee contributions, and some 217 children who received a medical check-up in the western city of Nashik in 2011.

- In Italy, country management is informed on a quarterly basis on the progress of projects using a set of key performance indicators. In common with other countries, nongovernmental organizations are required to report fully on the effectiveness of their partnership programs with ABB.

- ABB has an innovative scheme in Brazil in which children aged between 7 and 16 are brought into schools set up at factories in Sao Paulo, and given an extra half day of tuition and medical care as a way of preparing them for a working life. Success here can measured by the number of children who go on to a better life and jobs once they reach the age of 16.

At a corporate level, more than 80 students from around the world have now received scholarships from the ABB Jürgen Dormann Foundation for Engineering Education, which helps engineering students in need of financial support. Students from Malaysia entered the program in 2011, joining colleagues from Brazil, China, India, Mexico, Poland, Turkey and Vietnam in the scheme. The program is expected to be extended to other countries in 2012. Students on the program will come together in August 2012 at the second international meeting of foundation scholars in Switzerland. A film about the foundation's work is also being produced in 2012. Turning to corporate partnerships, ABB renewed its six-year agreement to support the Geneva-based International Committee of the Red Cross (ICRC) at the end of 2011. It is the company's largest corporate sponsorship.

Under the agreement, ABB will contribute financially to the ICRC's Water and Habitat program, which supports people in water-stressed areas and countries, and provides emergency accommodation to people caught up in zones of conflict. In 2012, ABB's funds are being used to support water programs in the Democratic Republic of Congo and Iraq.

ABB has benefited from training sessions given by ICRC specialists on humanitarian law and crisis management, as well as informal exchanges. In 2011, ABB engineers contributed to a training session on electromechanical engineering for ICRC staff members in Geneva.

They also continued our partnership agreement with WWF, the global conservation organization. There are four ongoing projects with WWF, two of which formally started in 2011. ABB in India is partnering with WWF to set up a solar-charged battery project in West Bengal for people to recharge their electrical goods; and in South Africa, solar panels were installed at a center for orphans of HIV/Aids victims.

In another project, a joint energy-efficiency training program for Chinese industry representatives has been held in five cities, including Beijing and Shanghai, with around 330 people taking part.

ABB's common efforts continue to focus on our "Access to Electricity" rural electrification program in India and Tanzania, which is strengthening the economic, social and environmental development of people in remote communities.

In Tanzania, ABB has partnered with local authorities and WWF to provide electricity to a village in the south of the country. The benefits of increased access to electricity have been marked and measurable. They include more schooling after dark, the health clinic being able to treat patients for more hours a day and the start of new businesses such as an electric sawmill and an oilseed press which are raising incomes and supporting better environmental management.

And in the Indian state of Rajasthan, ABB has partnered with an NGO and state authorities to bring distributed solar power to a widespread desert community. Some 8,000 people are benefiting from increased earnings because of the ability to work after dark, increased access to health care and more schooling. Tailors and weavers, for example, are earning up to 50 percent more because they can work at night, and the number of children attending school has doubled.

In these and other projects, ABB seeks to make a difference to the communities where we operate. We will continue to build on such concept with further engagement and contributions.

Security and crisis management

ABB Corporate Security focuses on processes, instructions and training to protect personnel and other assets from danger, loss or crime. As an integrated part of the ABB business, the security network analyzes threats and asset vulnerabilities in order to anticipate threats and mitigate risks. ABB has strengthened its security capability considerably in recent years with additional company and external experts in different parts of the world. The nature of risk has grown, and now potentially includes such diverse categories as war and terror, political upheaval, environmental hazards and natural disasters, different kinds of crime, and business intelligence and maritime threats.

One of the recent areas of focus has been on travel security. ABB has a system in place which tracks traveling employees globally and can be used to notify travelers and management of risks and dangerous situations as they occur. In times of crisis ABB Corporate Security can provide advice and support in relocating vulnerable staff and assets. By the end of 2011, about 850 managers in all eight regions, we well as almost all country management teams, had been trained on crisis management with workshops and exercises.

ABB strengthened its due diligence on security companies with a global program started in 2011 to ensure all such companies meet ABB and international standards. Work on the program will continue in 2012. New Group-wide security guidelines are also being drawn up, based on the Voluntary Principles for Security and Human Rights, They are due to be finalized in 2012.

Governance and integrity: Guiding our growth

During 2011, ABB released ambitious new growth targets for our business, aiming to increase revenues for 2011 to 2015 organically at a compound annual growth rate of 7–10 percent, with the potential for an additional 3–4 percentage points of growth by acquisition.

The achievement of such targets will be challenging, and is supported by programs in all areas of our business. These programs include work to ensure that sustainability considerations and values are a seamless part of our business practice along the value chain. Growth on this scale will also not be possible unless our behavior is firmly guided by our business principles of responsibility, respect and determination.

Standards of business conduct: ABB integrity program

ABB sets high standards of integrity, which are expected of every employee and in every country where we do business. We use a systematic approach, supported by tools and processes and a zero tolerance policy for violations.

Integrity is driven by the businesses with division heads and financial controllers regularly reviewing and reporting on integrity developments. The divisions' business performance evaluations also include consideration of integrity.

The ABB Code of Conduct is the integrity framework that describes the behavior expected of employees and stakeholders. It contains practical instructions to help employees in their day-to-day work and is underpinned by standards and policies covering issues such as corruption and illegal payments.

The Code of Conduct has been translated into 45 languages. All current and new employees are required to take Code of Conduct face-to-face and e-learning training, and to acknowledge their commitment to adhere to the Code of Conduct. Managers also have to re-acknowledge the Code of Conduct on a regular basis.

Multiple channels are available to all employees to report integrity concerns. A multilingual Business Ethics Hotline is available 24 hours per day, seven days per week, run by a third party. Calls are treated confidentially and people with information can choose to remain anonymous. A Stakeholder Hotline is available to our external business partners.

ABB also has an Ombuds program as an additional route for integrity reporting. The ABB Ombudspersons are respected, experienced business colleagues available for discussion and to provide confidential guidance.

ABB investigates all potential integrity concerns and cooperates fully with law enforcement agencies. There is a strict zero tolerance policy for violations of the law or the ABB Code of Conduct, which is enforced through systematic disciplinary actions. Overall, the ABB integrity program is supported by a team of some 330 employees, full-time and part-time, at headquarters and around the world.

Other policies, principles and procedures

They have also implemented environmental, social, human rights, and health and safety policies and a Supplier Code of Conduct. These policies include references to international standards to which they relate. For example, the human rights and social policies draw on the Universal Declaration of Human Rights, the ILO Core Conventions on Labor Standards, UN Global Compact, the OECD Guidelines for Multinational Enterprises and the Social Accountability 8000 standard.

Sustainability governance

For ABB, sustainability is about balancing economic success, environmental stewardship and social progress to benefit all our stakeholders; to truly contribute to a better world.

Ultimately, every ABB employee is responsible for sustainability. The commitment of line managers to implement our objectives is key to achieving ABB's sustainability and business goals. As part of our 2011 review of sustainability strategy, in alignment with the Group strategy review, we reinforced ABB's sustainability governance structure. A Sustainability Board, comprising the ABB Executive Committee, will now be accountable for the sustainability performance of ABB. The Sustainability Board will oversee sustainability policies and programs, to ensure consistency with business goals and ambitions and will monitor progress towards our targets.

The ABB Sustainability Affairs organization is responsible for the development and coordination of policies and programs covering health and safety, environment, corporate responsibility, and security and crisis management. Sustainability Affairs reports directly to Executive Committee member Gary Steel.

A network of sustainability specialists worldwide reports to the Sustainability Affairs management team. In countries where ABB entities have or could have significant sustainability impacts, we have appointed country sustainability controllers, country health and safety advisors and country security managers responsible for ABB's sustainability management program and for gathering the data consolidated in this report. Where needed, regional responsibilities have also been assigned.

The country and regional specialists are supported by local sustainability officers and health and safety advisors. Overall, the sustainability network is supported by a team of some 800 employees, full-time and part-time, at headquarters and around the world.

Sustainability risks and opportunities are also investigated in coordination with business divisions and other Group functions, e.g. Mergers and Acquisitions (due diligence), Real Estate and Insurance (real estate liabilities, security and site risk), Internal Audit and ABB's bid evaluation committee (customer and project risk assessments). They aim to cover all ABB Group companies, wholly owned subsidiaries and majority-owned joint ventures worldwide that might have significant sustainability impacts, with ABB's formal sustainability reporting system. Integration of Baldor Electric Company, acquired in January 2011, is continuing. For 2011, they have collected environmental data for Baldor covering water, energy and waste parameters. Data collection for other environmental parameters, health and safety and corporate responsibility will be implemented during 2012.

The data in this report relating to social performance cover 89 percent of ABB employees, whereas data relating to environmental performance cover 85 percent of employees. The environmental performance of the remaining 15 percent of employees, located in non-manufacturing entities without significant impacts, is covered by estimated data.

They use three computerized data reporting questionnaires to measure and collect performance data throughout the Group via the ABB intranet – an annual social report from every country, an annual environment report from every site and a monthly health and safety report from every country.

Externally developed charters, principles and initiatives

ABB subscribes to externally developed charters and principles for sustainability management. Applying such principles is helping ABB to make progress in core areas. These charters and principles include the International Chamber of Commerce Business Charter for Sustainable Development, which ABB signed in 1992, and ISO 14000 standards and technical reports.

ABB has adopted ISO 14001 for environmental management systems; ISO/TR 14025 for Environmental Product Declarations; ISO 14040-45 for Life Cycle Assessments; and ISO 19011 for environmental auditing of organizations.

ABB has incorporated the principles of OHSAS 18001, the International Labour Organization (ILO) guidelines on occupational health and safety management systems, and the ILO Code of Practice on Recording and Notification of Occupational Accidents and Diseases into its health and safety program.

ABB facilities are encouraged to implement integrated management systems for environmental and quality issues, and for occupational health and safety. Almost 250 sites now use integrated systems, many of which have been externally certified.

ABB is a signatory to the World Economic Forum's "Partnering Against Corruption Initiative" (PACI), signed by 170 companies committed to strengthening efforts to counter corruption and bribery.

In addition, ABB has taken note of the UN Guiding Principles on Business and Human Rights and is using its recommendations to assess expectations of corporate behavior.

As a founder member of the United Nations Global Compact, ABB has been closely involved in its development. ABB's understanding of human rights and day-to-day business benefits from involvement in such organizations.

6.4   CASE STUDY II: CE PRACTICES AT MAHINDRA AND MAHINDRA

Mahindra Group comprises many companies bound together by a common purpose and core values. The businesses are diversified across 18 key industry verticals spread across 5 continents and nearly 100 countries. The challenge of adopting a unified approach that would suit all our businesses was addressed by creating a cohesive structure for defining common principles and management of the journey. Our Group Sustainability Council developed a common set of commitments for businesses to chart the way forward. While the target was 10 certi☐ cations the on-ground results were 30. While the target was to reduce speci☐ c energy consumption by 2% in three years and 5% in ☐ ve, they clocked an 17.13% at the end of the third. Similar success was chalked up in water consumption with a 13.45% reduction in three years against targets of 2% in three years and 5% in ☐ ve. Alternative thinking has instilled in the employees' con☐ dence to aim and achieve higher. They aspire to achieve targets, and strive to surpass the competitors. The congruence of generating economic, social and environmental wealth has lent higher purpose to each member of Mahindra.

Over this ☐ ve year sustainability journey powered by the engine of Alternative Thinking, they have ingrained sustainable resource ef☐ ciency as a top business priority. They have

nurtured and helped blossom an innate ability to transform challenges into opportunities and forged stronger bonds not only with our customers and shareholders but also with the environment and society.

The un☐ inching belief in the core values, our unrelenting commitment to social empowerment and unwavering practice of sound governance has made us a stronger organisation. In 2008-09, we had created a Sustainability Roadmap for each of the businesses covered in the Sustainability Report in that year. This roadmap articulated goals over 3 and 5 year time horizons, with seven commitments.

Environmental sustainability

It is no surprise therefore that the year 2011-12 has been yet another year of achievement on all aspects of the triple bottom line. The profits were creditable, with the Group PAT rising from INR 38,172.83 million to INR 54,103 million. More importantly, they also devoted time, sustainable resources and energy towards the planet and the people. On the environment front, the foray in renewable energy materialized, as Mahindra Solar One commissioned its first 5 MW solar power plant, as a part of the Jawaharlal Nehru National Solar Mission. This project holds the distinction of generating the highest output per MW of any solar plant in India. This is a small beginning that reiterates the belief that creating shared value for communities and corporates is the way of the future.

Product flexibility

On the product front, the global debut of the XUV5OO was a success. This product is not only chic and beautifully designed but fuel-friendly, in accordance with our emphasis on sustainability. The commitment to inclusive growth and delivering Farm-Tech Prosperity was further strengthened through a variety of new agri-initiatives that impact the lives of farmers, enabling them to rise above their current realm of possibility. The financial services expanded into products designed specifically for rural financial inclusion extends social sustainability. The real estate business is looking at making affordable and sustainable housing, a priority area. And these are just a few high points of the performance; many more are detailed in this report.

Green policy

The CEO believes this is only the beginning of our sustainability journey. The sustainability goals are not destinations - they are check posts that enable us to increase our efforts, to reinvest new opportunities and to renew commitments for a better tomorrow. Our performance so far, will encourage us to set higher targets and to achieve faster sustainable growth.

At Mahindra, they see sustainability as a competitive advantage. Since they embarked on this journey in 2007-08, they have learnt a lot and have progressed from intentions to commitments to actions. The principles of sustainability have taken firm root in their businesses and by applying 'Alternative Thinking', we have enabled ourselves to accelerate results across the economic, social and environmental bottom lines.

Mahindra Group comprises many companies bound together by a common purpose and core values. The businesses are diversified across 18 key industry verticals spread across 5 continents and nearly 100 countries. The challenge of adopting a unified approach that would suit all our businesses was addressed by creating a cohesive structure for defining common principles and management of the journey. The Group developed a common set of commitments for businesses to chart the way forward.

- **Completeness** The Report presents Mahindra's sustainability performance for its Group companies that contribute to more than 85% of its annual turnover. This year the new companies included in the reporting boundary are as follows: Mahindra Reva Electric Vehicles Private Limited, Mahindra Rural Housing Finance Limited, Mahindra Insurance Brokers Limited, Mahindra First Choice Wheels Limited and Mahindra Solar One Private Limited.

- **Balance** The Report adequately presents the positive and negative aspects of Mahindra's sustainability performance.

- **Comparability** Year-on-year trends related to key sustainability performance indicators for last three years have been presented in the Report. Across Group

141

companies, Mahindra has presented specific consumption values for water, energy and GHG emissions.

- **Accuracy** The sustainability data and information presented in the Report has been collected, collated and analysed by Mahindra's Corporate Sustainability Cell. During the verification visits, data transcription and calculation errors were detected and resolved. Overall, the data and information presented in the final version of the Report are well within accepted margins of error and along with appropriate presentation of underlying assumptions and techniques.

- **Timeliness** Mahindra follows a regular schedule for publication of this Report. The Corporate Sustainability Cell conducts interim checks and balances on the data and information submitted by the Group companies to ensure quality and consistency.

- **Clarity** Appropriate use of graphics and data tables make the data and information presented in the Report easy to search and understand.

- **Reliability** The collection and collation process for sustainability data and information at Mahindra is partly through an online portal and partly through manual worksheets. During the reporting period the online portal could only manage quantitative data. Overall, the sustainability data and information presented in the Report are reliable; however the process to establish the reliability is cumbersome.

- **GRI Application Level Check** The report meets the criteria set for A+ application level.

Table 7.2: Summary of the case findings

Issues	M&M	ABB
Green policy	M	H
Green human sustainable resource Management	H	H
Green technology	M	H
Green supply chain management	H	H
Green product flexibility	H	M

Note: M-Moderate; H-High; L-Low; this is on the basis of 6 point scale where 0-1.99=low; 2-3.99=Moderate; 4-6=High.

At M&M, management facilitated sustainability by rewarding employees for adopting sustainability practices, providing flexibility to the employees to decide which material they want to use, how much product can be initiated so that the green emission is minimized. It generated ideas by updating and expanding employees' knowledge bases, thus increasing the organizational knowledge. High level of management support resulted into better results adoption of sustainability efforts.

6.6 CONCLUDING REMARKS

Implemented practices for two cases from manufacturing sector have been studied and presented in this chapter. From these case studies, we can conclude that M&M and ABB are displaying sustainability characteristics. It emerges that while encouraging sustainability; the internal environment should be decided after careful consideration of relation and sustainable interplay of contextual factors comprising it.

At M&M, management has been able to facilitate sustainability by rewarding employees for sustainability, providing work discretion to the employees' product flexibility, providing management support for green supply chain management. Further as a part of our analysis, we found out that between the two case studies, ABB is more sustainable than M&M. Due to the presence of conducive environmental parameters; these companies were successful in adopting sustainable practices.

CHAPTER 7

SYNTHESIS OF LEARNINGS - MODEL FOR SUSTAINABILITY[•]

7.1   INTRODUCTION

Globalisation has heralded burgeoning ship movements and maritime **operations** in ports alongside increased international concerns regarding potential environmental impacts. In particular, smaller ports require accessible tools to manage them. A framework to facilitate environmental **management** applies business process principles to identify relevant inputs, processes and outputs. A case study of Falmouth Harbour Commissioners compares functional units and flows that define input-output processes for anchoring and bunkering operations. Strategic-level processes affect present and future operations while tactical service processes guarantee service level and quality through their integrity. Operational processes occur at the output level. An accessible generic framework supports planning of more sustainable maritime operations, facilitates mitigation of potential risks and encourages authorities to engage with sustainability agendas and manage development proposals proactively. Ongoing interlocution with business strategists will refocus port managers on educational and commercial missions and increase stakeholder engagement. Simplification and optimisation phases of business process re-engineering remain untapped by business strategists.

Part of this chapter is to be published as:

Bhardwaj, B.R., Mangal, V. (Ann) and Lai, Kee-hung (2013) Impact of Green Policy on Ecologically Sustainable Organization: A Study in Emerging Market Context, Accepted for publication in International Journal of Global Business Competitiveness, 2013.

The methodology mentioned in section 6.2 has been used for the case studies in service organizations undertaken in this chapter. For the sake of brevity, the same has not been mentioned here. The two organizations and their practices were selected on the basis of purposive sampling. The data was gathered through observations, literature available on these companies and questionnaire based interviews from these organizations. The various practices and the actions taken by these organizations have been studied in detail. The learnings have been presented in this chapter.

7.2   SYNTHESIS OF RESEARCH FINDINGS

7.2.1   Introduction

A conceptual framework was evolved in chapter three (Figure 3.1) for sustainability practice on the basis of the research evidences from the literature survey. Based on the conceptual model, the dimensions for each part of the model were identified on the basis of literature survey. The variables were enriched on the basis of the findings of the pilot study of four cases from select organizations as presented in chapter four. These variables formed the basis of the questionnaire used in the survey study administered in services and manufacturing organizations (chapter five).

The learning's from questionnaire survey studies and the case studies are compared to bring out the commonality and support from one study to the 'weak variables' of the other study. The organizational antecedents selected have been synthesized and are grouped on the basis of the conceptual framework, thus giving the 'Sustainability Model'.

The Sustainable SAP analysis presents the situation, actor, and process study of the Infosys Technologies Ltd.

Prevailing Situation

Opportunities

- There is a vast potential for companies to become competitive through sustainability efforts.

- There is a huge demand for sustainability practices including environmental and social sustainability.

- Government of India enforcing 2% of the profits to be dedicated to social responsibilities.

Threats

- There are many organizations providing similar services to the society.

- Globalization, new regulations, technology, and change in demographics posed a huge challenge for the company in this area.

Actors

- The key actors include the managers, top management, NGOs, government, society.

- According to the analysis, a major 42.3% of the respondents rated 4 on the scale, i.e., they have clear defined definition of the environmental policy of their store. 28% have explicitly defined their policy and 23.9% have an average idea about the policy. Only 4.8% of people have unclear idea regarding the policy, and none of the respondents (0%) have rated 1, i.e., don't have any environmental policy at all. This shows that there are hardly any or a very few companies these days who ignore their responsibility towards the environment and frame policies to ensure a sustainable development.

- According to the analysis maximum no. of respondents (45.3%) have an absolutely clear cut idea about the objectives and long term environmental plans for their business. An encouraging 40.5% of companies also have a good idea about the short term and long term plans. Only a mere 7.1% of respondents don't have any concrete objectives and plans regarding the environment, and rest 2.4% and 4.8% of respondents have poor to average have a lucid plan for the same.

Processes

- **Green human sustainable resource management:**
  - o Well-defined environmental responsibilities: According to the analysis, a maximum of 57% of companies admitted to have a very clear cut idea about their environmental responsibilities whereas only 7% of companies admitted to have no environmental responsibilities at all. Companies with an excellent idea of such responsibilities comprised of 26% which has enabled them to adopt sustainable practices.
  - Full-time employees devoted to environmental management: According to the analysis a disappointing majority of 48% of companies don't have specialized employees for environmental management, even though a considerable percentage of respondents have projected to show concern about sustainability. Further 26% of respondents have full-time employees devoted to this department and 16% of companies have an excellent group of employees working for the same.

- Natural environment training programmes for managers and employees: Again from this analysis, we have deduced that a majority of 48% respondents don't have any environment training programmes for managers or employees. Sadly there are no respondents (0%) who have regular and effective workshops or programmes regarding environment sensitization of the employees. Nearly 5% of respondents have sporadic or poor system for training and only 12% have a good training system in hand.

- **Environmental policy**

- Systems for measuring and assessing environmental performance: From this analysis, we deduced that majority of respondents (36%) have a fairly average system for measuring and assessing environmental performance and 24% of respondents have poor control system. Sadly 26% of respondents have no such system at all and none of the respondents have any dedicated environmental control system.

- Environmental emergency plans: According to the analysis a majority of respondents (60%) don't have any environmental emergency plans at all. Around 10% of respondents have insufficient and fairly good plans for tackling with such emergencies alike. Also disappointingly none of the respondents had any clear-cut or articulate emergency plan.

- Periodic elaboration of environmental reports: According to the analysis a majority of the respondents rated 1 on the, i.e., don't undergo periodic evaluation of environmental reports at all. 31% of the companies evaluate the environmental reports time and again. About 10% of the companies rarely evaluate such reports and about 5% of the companies undergo consistent evaluation. Only a minority of 2% of respondents undergo rigorous periodic evaluation of environmental reports.

- **Green supply chain management**
- Environmental criteria in supplier selection: According to the analysis 24% of respondents don't consider environmental criteria in selecting their supplier. Around 7% of respondents give both negligible though as well as well as have strict environmental criteria for selecting supplier. Around 40.5% of the respondents have a good concern for supplier selection and about 21.55 of respondents have average criteria for supplier selection.
- Shipments consolidation: According to the analysis, about 38% of the respondents considered environmental factors during shipment consolidation averagely. About 29% of the respondents didn't consider any environmental concerns over shipment consolidation and about 26% of them had some serious concern over shipment consolidations. Only about 5% of the respondents confirmed to have strict criteria over shipment and a minority of about 2% admitted to have very slight considerations over shipment consolidation.
- Selection of cleaner transportation methods: About a majority of respondents (42%) rated that they take selection of cleaner transportation pretty seriously and about 29% of the respondents take the selection generally. About 21% of the respondents take special care and are extra cautious about selection on transportation method and about 5% of them

gives it very little thought. Only about 2% of the respondents don't bother for energy efficient and cleaner mode of transportation at all.

- Recyclable or reusable packaging or container in logistics: According to the analysis maximum number of the respondents i.e., the companies, recycle or re-use packaging or container in logistics, the percentage is 52.4%. very less percentage (7.1%) of companies don't recycle or re-use the packaging. This shows that companies minimize wastage and promote recycling. About 4.8% of companies re-use very less packaging.

- Ecological materials for primary packaging: About a majority of respondents (54.8%) rated that they use ecological material for primary packaging most of the time and about 19.1% of the respondents do not use any eco friendly material in their primary packaging of products. Only 7.1% of the respondents use very less ecological material for primary packaging and about 10% of them us ecological material for packaging almost all the time.

- Supplier and NGO cooperation in carbon labeling: According to the analysis, a maximum of 50% of the respondents have never got any support from suppliers and NGOs in carbon labeling. Only 5% of the respondents have an excellent cooperation system from suppliers and NGOs.

- Green procurement: According to the analysis, a maximum of 42% of the respondents follow green procurement in an efficient way and frequently. About 26% never do any green procurement. Only 2.4% of the respondents always go for green procurement.

- Green packaging: According to the analysis, a maximum of 50% of the respondents do green packaging at a very good rate. About 2% of the respondents have never done any green packaging. 24% of the respondents always go green packaging which is eco-friendly.

- **Green technology**

- Recuperation and recycling system : According to the analysis, about 35.8% of the respondents recovered through the recycling system most of the time. About 9.6% of the respondents don't go for recycling system at all. Around 17% of respondents have systematic and coherent recycling system.

- Acquisition of clean technology/equipment: According to the analysis, about 42.3% of the respondents have acquired or bought most of the clean equipment or the machinery relating to their field. Interestingly, there was no retailer who didn't invest in any form of green technology or equipment. This shows that companies are also spending money on cleaner technology.

- Designs focused on reducing sustainable resource consumption and waste generation during production and distribution: According to the analysis, a maximum of 29% of the companies used designs focused on reducing sustainable resource consumption and waste generation during production and distribution quiet efficiently. Only 7.1% of the respondents were very regular and strict to use green and environmentally efficient designs focused all the time. Sadly, around 21% of them don't make use of such designs at all.

- Design focused on reducing sustainable resource consumption and waste generation in product usage: According to the analysis, a maximum of 40.5% of the companies made average use of designs focused on reducing sustainable resource consumption and waste generation in product usage. About 21% of the respondents did not use any such designs. About 12% of the respondents use such designs very occasionally and very frequently.

- Design for disassembly, reusability and recyclability: According to the analysis, a maximum of 40.5% of the companies made good use of designs focused for disassembly, reusability and recyclability. 10% of the respondents used such designs on a regular basis. About 12% of the respondents always use and the same percentage of companies use them only sometimes.

- Emission filters and end-of-pipe control: According to the analysis, a maximum of 54.8% of the respondents never used emission filters and end-of-pipe control. None of the respondents admitted to use them on a strictly regular basis. But about 17% have effectively made use of emission filters.

- Process design focused on reducing energy and natural sustainable resources consumption in operations: According to the analysis, a maximum of 31% of the respondents always and sometimes use process design focused on reducing energy and natural sustainable resources consumption in operations. 12% of the respondents never use such process designs.

- Enhance water and energy conservation: According to the analysis, a maximum of 48% of the respondents put very good efforts to enhance water and energy conservation. About 5% of the respondents never did anything to enhance water and energy conservation in their retail outlet. About 36% of the respondents have a dedicated system for water and energy conservation.

- **Product flexibility**
- The organization allows rule bending except that everybody is expected to follow a code of conduct. The organization takes on the responsibility to develop an environment which the people enjoy and are productive and cause the organization to grow. The informal rules related to financial performance are adaptable to the situation. The expectation is that the managers are always informed about the concept. People are allowed to break rules as far as the concept are based on common sense. The organization is flexible to accommodate the deviations from published policies as far as they are supported by common sense and has been done to meet customers' orders.
- Environmental arguments in marketing: According to the evaluation a majority of respondents (48%) don't go for environmental arguments in green marketing, i.e., green marketing. Around 21% of the companies put forth a rather strong environmental argument while marketing their products or schemes. About a 19% of the companies use green marketing to a fairly good extent and about 5% of the companies draw on green marketing rarely. Only 7% of respondents use excessive green marketing techniques for their retail outlets or franchises.

- Having flexibility in sponsoring of environmental events/collaboration with ecological organization: According to the analysis, a major chunk of companies i.e 67% of the respondents did not sponsor any kind of event with any ecological organization. An equal proportion of the respondents sponsored events with the ecological organizations at various level ranging from average to very frequent, the percentage being 7.1%.

- Substitution of polluting and hazardous materials/parts: According to the analysis, a major chunk of companies i.e., 55% of the respondents had moderately substituted hazardous materials. Equal number of the respondents procured or replaced hazardous parts as and when required and also replaced very occasionally, the percentage being 7%.

- Product planning and control focused on reducing waste and optimization materials exploitation: According to the analysis, a maximum of 45.3% of the respondents have an effective product planning and control focused on reducing waste and optimization materials exploitation. About 29% never did any product planning and control focused. Only about 17% of the respondents have a thorough and systematic plan for product planning.

- Adopt green store design for energy conservation and utilization: According to the analysis, a maximum of 33% of the respondents have a very good green store design for energy conservation and utilization. About 21% of the respondents never adopted any green store design. Only 7% of the respondents have a little or minimal focus for green store design and 14% have an excellent green store design.

- **Sustainability strategy**

- Regular voluntary information about environmental management to customers and institutions: According to the analysis, a major chunk of companies i.e., 45% did not provide any kind of regular and voluntary information about environmental management to the customers and institutions. Only 4.8% of the respondents provided frequent and periodic information about their environmental management to customers.

- Preference for green products in purchasing: According to the analysis, a maximum of 26% of the companies mostly prefer the green products in purchasing quiet frequently. About 19% are the ones who always prefer green products. Sadly, 23.9% of the companies never prefer for green products in purchasing.

- Responsible disposal of waste and residues (separation and preparation): According to the analysis, a maximum of 35.8% of the respondents undergo the disposal of waste and residues (separation and preparation) of the products after use very frequently or at a very good rate. About 10% of the respondents don't go for such systems at all. 24% of the respondents are very sincere in their efforts to dispose waste properly and effectively.

- Reduces green house gas emission: According to the analysis, a maximum of 26% of the respondents have a very good focus on reducing green house gas emission through various methods. About 17% of the respondents do nothing to reduce green house gas emission and 245 do everything they can to reduce emissions of carbon dioxide and other harmful gasses.

7.2.4   LAP Synthesis

The LAP synthesis presents the learning, action and performance analysis of M&M and ABB. The data collected has been analyzed and interpreted with respect to sustainability. Some of the qualitative aspects of internal environment for adopting sustainability practices are mentioned below:

- The organization emphasizes on having well-defined environmental responsibilities. Companies with an excellent idea of such responsibilities comprised of 26% which has enabled them to adopt sustainable practices.

- The companies adopting sustainable practices have systems for measuring and assessing environmental performance and designed objective for departmental goals to be achieved in sustaibility (e.g. case study of M&M, and ABB).

- Enhancing Green supply chain management has helped to align the suppliers contribution in reducing carbon footprints and emission. This can be also enhances through Shipments consolidation, Selection of cleaner transportation methods, Recyclable or reusable packaging or container in logistics, Ecological materials for primary packaging, Supplier and NGO cooperation in carbon labeling, Green procurement, and Green packaging.

- Adoption of Green technology cab be done through Recuperation and recycling system, Acquisition of clean technology/equipment, Designs focused on reducing sustainable resource consumption and waste generation during production and distribution, Design focused on reducing sustainable resource consumption and waste generation in product usage, Design for disassembly, reusability and recyclability, Emission filters and end-of-pipe control, Process design focused on reducing energy and natural sustainable resources consumption in operations, and by Enhancing water and energy conservation.

- Product flexibility provided scope for sustaibility by having flexibility for collaboration with ecological organization, flexibility in substitution of polluting and hazardous materials/parts, flexibility in product planning and control focused on reducing waste and optimization materials exploitation, flexibility in adopting green store design for energy conservation and utilization,

7.2.5 Performance

The performance of the sustainability efforts is measured in terms of various strategy including regular voluntary information about environmental management to customers and institutions, Responsible disposal of waste and residues, and reduction in green house gas emission. The study suggests that companies adopting green sustaibility practices also impact the customers and the customers and shareholders have a better image about the company. This in turn influences the goodwill of the company and share and market price of the company and the profits too.

7.5 CONCLUDING REMARKS

Implemented strategies for two cases from services sector have been studied and presented in this chapter. It emerges that the internal drivers for sustainability practice should be decided after careful consideration of relation and sustainable interplay of contextual factors relating to the internal work environment. The various processes adopted by these organizations have helped to achieve better sustainability strategy.

CHAPTER 8

SUMMARY

8.1 INTRODUCTION

The synthesis of the learning issues is discussed in this chapter in the context of sustainable business environment. The results and findings of the research study are summarized and some suggestions are made for organizations, particularly for managers who want to practice sustainability within the organizations. The support for the results/findings of the study from recent published literature is also presented. Further, significant research contributions, implications for researchers and practitioners, limitations of the study, and the possible directions for the future work are outlined.

8.2 SUMMARY OF MAJOR FINDINGS

Relationships of Key Variables

The relationships of key research variables have been established by both the questionnaire survey and the case studies and the research findings on this front are summarized as follows:

- The case studies reveal that the environmental policy for plays an important role for stimulating sustaibility strategy within the organization.

* Part of this chapter has been published as:
Bhardwaj, B.R., Sushil, Momaya, K. (2011) Case Studies of Social Entrepreneurship in Indian Context: SAP-LAP Learning Critical Success Factors, *International Journal of Economics Management and Engineering* (IJEME), Volume 2 - Issue 2/3, pp. 231 – 251.

- The case studies also show that development of business-relevant KPIs and objectives, in consultation with the businesses and functions enhances the sustaibility strategy significantly. The focus could be on sustainable resource efficiency.

- Green product development including developing world-class products, systems and services to lower our customers' energy use, reduce their emissions and improve sustainable resource efficiency on a long-term basis can enhance the sustaibility strategy significantly.

- Ensuring the operations are energy and sustainable resource efficient can also enhance the sustaibility strategy significantly.

- Green supplier selection through proactively ensuring suppliers, employees and business partners work in a safe, healthy and secure environment, and to the highest standards of integrity, and Supplier Sustainability Development Program can enhance the sustaibility strategy significantly.

- Strengthening employees' involvement and commitment through green human sustainable resource development can improve the company's sustainability performance.

- Social sustaibility parameters can be development of human rights standards, ensuring Freedom of engagement, Health and safety, Equality of opportunity, Compensation, Working hours, Community involvement, and designing policy for Business ethics.

- Environmental sustaibility can be achieved by Sustainability in the supply chain, developing Supplier Code of Conduct (The code need to cover supplier performance in fair and legal labor conditions, occupational health and safety, environmental responsibility and business ethics, poor waste disposal practices, or a lack of appropriate protective equipment for workers).

On the basis of detailed analysis and synthesis the following diagram is shown in figure 8.1. The figure explains the relationships between the drivers and strategy.

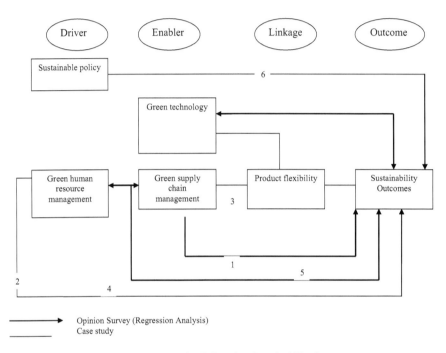

Figure 8.1 Validated Conceptual Framework for Enhancing Sustainability Strategy

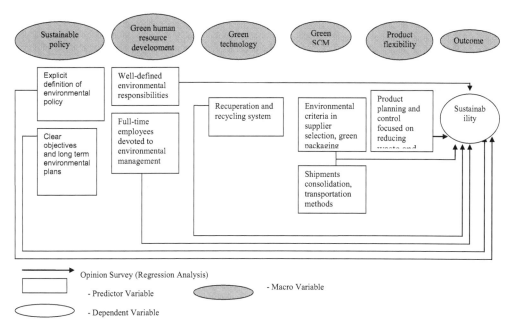

Figure 8.2: Validated Model for Micro Variable of Environmental Sustainability

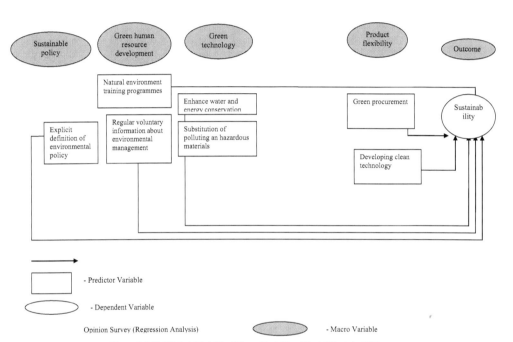

Figure 8.3: Validated Model for Micro Variable of Social Sustainability

Table 8.2: Synthesis of Influencing Relationships for Sustainability

Relationship No.	Influencing Practice	Practice Area being Influenced by the Relationship	Influence Relationship Description
1	Sustainable policy	Designing of explicit definition of environmental policy	Enhancing sustainability by designing clear objectives and long term environmental plans
2	Green human sustainable resource management	Employee motivation for sustainable practices	Enhancing employee commitment towards sustainable concept by management support and by designing well-defined environmental responsibilities
3	Green technology	Motivation of employees to design recuperation and recycling system and cleaner technology	Rewarding employees for cleaner technology innovations
4	Green supply chain management	Collaborating with suppliers for adopting clean transportation methods	Collaboration and guidance in co-developing the cleaner methods of packaging and transportation
5	Product flexibility	Interdepartmental collaboration and cross-functional teams for product flexibility	Increasing interdepartmental collaboration enhances sustainability strategy

Note: The major predictors are given in italics. Refer to Figure 8.1.

Moreover, the management should provide support for these concept in terms of financial and promotional support by recognizing such efforts. Further, it should also provide the direction, scope and sustainable resources for achieving sustainable targets as discussed in the case studies. The details of these linkages are given in Figure 8.1. This figure includes the linkages from the findings of the regression analysis (questionnaire survey study).

The inter linkages of the different organizational antecedents have been explored further through case studies which have helped to understand the overall implications of these linkages for practice of sustaibility concept within the organizations.

The synthesis of the Sustainability Model macro variable is given in Table 8.2, which explains the impact of these variables on sustainability strategy in terms of driving influence, by the relationship and the description of the relationship. The variables have been discussed according to the importance, which has emerged from regression analysis, and case studies. The similar order has also been followed in Figure 8.1. Then the interaction between organizational antecedents affecting the sustainability strategy has been given. The detailed interpretation of these relationships is explained as follows:

Sustainable policy
Sustainable policy directly affects the environmental and social sustaibility strategy. Sustainable policy has emerged as a major predictor of environmental and social sustaibility. Having explicit definition of environmental policy and clear objectives and long term environmental plans affect the Environmental Sustainability. Moreover, explicit definition of environmental policy also influences Social Sustainability directly. These links were observed in macro analysis (step-wise regression analysis) of questionnaire survey given in chapter five. Thus, it can be concluded that Sustainable

policy can be utilized as a major organizational antecedent to improve the Sustainability strategy.

Green human sustainable resource development

The macro variable, Green human sustainable resource development, is acting as major driver of sustainability strategy. It also impacts the environmental sustainability. The analysis of micro variables led to the conclusion that Employee motivation for sustainable practices for adoption of sustainable practices. Thus, it can be concluded that Green human sustainable resource development can be utilized as a major organizational antecedent to improve the sustainability strategy. This is because enhancing employee commitment towards sustainable concept by management support and by designing well-defined environmental responsibilities.

Green technology

Green technology has emerged as a major driver, which affects the sustainability Strategy in terms of environmental sustainability and social sustainability. The regression analysis of micro variables (given in chapter six) shows that Green technology in terms of Rewarding employees for cleaner technology innovations affects environmental sustainability and social sustainability significantly. Thus, it can be concluded that Green technology can be utilized as a major organizational antecedent to improve the sustainability strategy.

Green supply chain management

Through the step-wise regression analysis, it emerged that Collaborating with suppliers for adopting clean transportation methods is acting as a driver of sustainability. It is evident from the framework (Figure 8.3) that Collaborating with suppliers has higher order of impact on environmental sustainability and social sustainability in terms of co-developing the cleaner methods of packaging and transportation. Thus, it can be concluded that Collaborating with suppliers can be utilized as a major organizational antecedent to improve the sustainability strategy in terms of environmental sustainability and social sustainability, which has been practically experienced in questionnaire survey in 39 organizations from manufacturing and service sectors.

Product flexibility

The case study analyses have shown that Interdepartmental collaboration and cross-functional teams for product flexibility act as an enabler of sustainability concept (chapter six and seven).

8.3.1 Interpretive Matrix of Sustainability Model

The sustainability model shown in Figures 8.1 is interpreted and presented is shown as interpretive matrix (Sushil, 2005a). The interpretive matrix represents a set of relationships in a matrix form, giving interpretation for each paired relationship in the relevant cell.

	GP	GHRM	GT	GSCM	PF	SO
GP						
GHRM	Encouragement for sustainability					
GT	Sharing of risk and concerted efforts for developing cleaner technology	Inter organizational collaboration for providing training for adopting sustainable practices				
GSCM	Collaboration with suppliers	-	Enhances knowledge sharing on technology development			
PF	Green product development flexibility	More number of ideas for green product development	Expert contribution on expertise on green material	Enhancing the supply chain management		
SO	Designing explicit Environmental policy	Increase in number of process improvement through sustainable adoption	Increase in sustainable product improvement	Better products development with least emission and energy consumption	Focused product development	Increasing recycling, reuse
	GP	**GHRM**	**GT**	**GSCM**	**PF**	**SO**

Figure 8.4: Alliance Interpretive Matrix of Sustainability Strategy

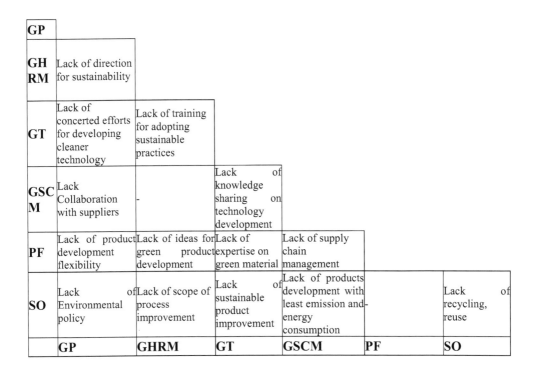

	GP	GHRM	GT	GSCM	PF	SO
GP						
GHRM	Lack of direction for sustainability					
GT	Lack of concerted efforts for developing cleaner technology	Lack of training for adopting sustainable practices				
GSCM	Lack Collaboration with suppliers	-	Lack of knowledge sharing on technology development			
PF	Lack of product development flexibility	Lack of ideas for green product development	Lack of expertise on green material	Lack of supply chain management		
SO	Lack of Environmental policy	Lack of scope of process improvement	Lack of sustainable product improvement	Lack of products development with least emission and energy consumption	-	Lack of recycling, reuse
	GP	**GHRM**	**GT**	**GSCM**	**PF**	**SO**

Figure 8.5: Conflict Interpretive Matrix of Sustainability Strategy

170

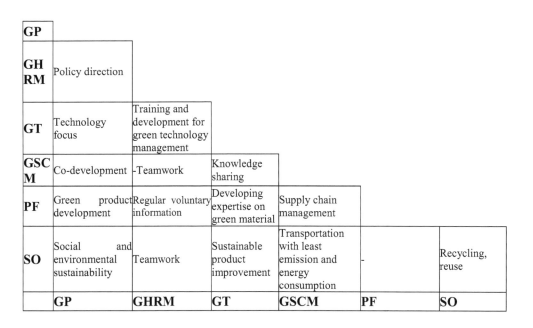

	GP	GHRM	GT	GSCM	PF	SO
GP						
GH RM	Policy direction					
GT	Technology focus	Training and development for green technology management				
GSC M	Co-development	-Teamwork	Knowledge sharing			
PF	Green product development	Regular voluntary information	Developing expertise on green material	Supply chain management		
SO	Social and environmental sustainability	Teamwork	Sustainable product improvement	Transportation with least emission and energy consumption	-	Recycling, reuse
	GP	**GHRM**	**GT**	**GSCM**	**PF**	**SO**

Figure 8.6: Synthesis of Interpretive Matrix for Sustainability Strategy

171

There are three basic types of interpretive matrices namely triangular, square and rectangular. A triangular matrix depicts undirected relations among a set of elements/variables, for example, self-interaction matrix, correlation matrix. A square interpretive matrix shows directed relationships among a set of elements/variables.

The relationship between a pair of element j, and i; two entries are made in the matrix; one depicting the directed relation from i to j; and other one from j to i. A rectangular matrix depicts relations between two sets of elements 'n' and 'm', for example, the cross-interaction matrix. If the number of elements in both sets is same, i.e., 'n' is equal to 'm', it physically appears to be a square matrix, but since the set of elements is different on both dimensions it is a special case of the rectangular matrix. This matrix represents undirected relations. This papers attempts to apply triangular matrix for understanding the determinants of sustainability.

In this empirical research, a 'triangular interpretive matrix' has been prepared for the undirected relations tested by univariate and multivariate analysis (given in chapter five and six). The significant correlations indicate possible association/relation for the respective pairs. The cells having significant correlations have been provided with the interpretation of relation, which provide a clue to the direction of relation in terms of dependent and independent variables. The correlation matrix and triangular interpretive matrix in the context of internal environmental factors of sustainability is shown in chapter five.

Based on the relationships depicted by Sustainability Model (Figure 8.1), two matrices were developed namely alliance matrix of sustainability strategy (Figure 8.4) and conflict matrix of CE strategy (Figure 8.5). Alliance matrix of Sustainability strategy describes the pros and conflict matrix describes the cons of the relationships. Further, based on the case studies (chapter seven and eight) Sheshadri et al. (2004), the various processes, which can take care of these relationships, have been mapped in the relevant boxes (Figure 8.6). The synthesis for practice implications has been given in Figure 8.6. This matrix explains the Sustainability Model in terms of overall impact and processes to better deal with the implementation of Sustainability.

The relationships as depicted by these matrices show that Green human sustainable resource management can enhance sustainability by providing 'providing training programmes' (Figure 8.3). Similarly, Green human sustainable resource management enables the employees to adopt the sustainable processes by allowing inter-organizational collaboration. The various processes which will help the organization to implement sustainability across boundary includes the processes to build strong ties between different stakeholders including the employees, NGOs, and suppliers. Thus, the focus of the organization should be to build team building exercises and individual awareness programmes to increase teamwork within the organization (Figure 8.6).

The application of interpretive matrix has helped to understand the managerial implications from strategic point of view. It clearly helped to define the roles and responsibilities and the domain of influence. It has also helped to bring out the supporting ideas behind which appropriate practices and processes could be developed to facilitate sustainability. The application of this tool has clearly brought out the directed and undirected relationships among the various factors in facilitating sustainability process. The study has shown the importance of Green human sustainable resource management and Green policy as a pivot variable, which act as a key variable to affect the sustainability strategy. Hence, green policy is one of the critical organizational antecedents of sustainability strategy.

8.4   CONCLUDING REMARKS

The learnings from various studies namely pilot study, questionnaire based survey study and case studies have been synthesized in this chapter. On the basis of the integrated learning, a sustainability model has been presented. This model has been based on the conceptual framework evolved from the research evidences from the published literature and validated by the findings of the questionnaire based survey study obtained through statistical analysis. The sustainability model has further been verified and refined on the basis of the learnings from the case studies.

Based on the practice macro-factors, influence diagrams have been presented which bring out the dependencies and complementary nature of various practices. It is found that sustainability practices are strongly influenced by the internal environmental factors. Organization level micro-practices have also been presented and their influence on Sustainability Strategy has been brought out.

Unique issues for sustainability practice in work environment, evolved from the case studies have also been presented. These have been evolved on the basis of the case studies of organizations, relevant for other organizations with respect to sustainability, implemented in sustainable business environment.

These specific issues related to sustainability and help the organization for sustainable revitalization (Volberda, 1998; Sushil, 2006). These specific issues also help us to address the issue of organization's lack of vitality which us one of the key aspects of the organization's sustainability. Thus, the variables and their inter-relationships (findings of the study) help to revitalize the ongoing process of sustainable innovation within the organization in terms of ongoing processes, which have been highlighted in this study.

CHAPTER 9

CONCLUSIONS

9.1 Introduction

The findings of different components of the research, i.e. questionnaire survey and case study analysis are synthesized according to the research objectives. The main research objective was to identify the organizational antecedents for sustainability strategy. Accordingly, a summary of the findings are presented here, reflecting upon the achievement of the research objectives. The study brings out that the framework for sustainability should be evolved keeping in view the project goals and the contextual factors namely internal environmental factors. Based on the research findings, important areas have been identified which are discussed in the following sections.

In view of the above research findings presented in earlier chapters, the following observations can be concluded:

- The case studies show that the organization structure affects the implementation of sustainability practices. The hierarchical organization structure does not help to promote sustainability. The organization structure which provides scope for flexibility to the employees is important for successful implementation of innovative practices such as sustainability practice.

- The case studies also show that appropriate sustainability control measures help to manage the risk associated with the sustainable efforts.

- The case studies reveal that having appropriate performance evaluation systems help to stimulate innovative sustainable behavior among the employees.

- The relationships of key research variables are consistent in terms of regression analysis of macro and micro variables in questionnaire survey as well as case studies. The major predictor in case of macro analysis of questionnaire included green policy, green technology and green supply chain management. Similar findings have been reported by various researchers including Lai et al. (2010). In micro analysis, it was found that two variables namely, product flexibility and green supply chain management emerged as enablers of sustainability outcome from the case studies.

- The regression analysis indicates that green policy has significant relationship between green human sustainable resource management and green technology adoption. The research findings suggest that open communication for fostering information sharing and empowerment has been proffered as a critical element for sustainable innovation.

9.2. Validated Conceptual Framework

The validated relationships at macro level helped in the development of the validated conceptual framework as envisaged in the objective of the research. The objective has been probed in depth at the micro level as well and a validated framework exhibiting relationships among micro variables has also been developed, which can safely be treated as the validated model brought out by this research. The key findings related to validated conceptual framework are as follows:

- The validated conceptual framework generated by questionnaire survey has been corroborated by the case studies to a great extent. The variations in questionnaire survey are corroborated by micro level analysis of questionnaire survey.

- Although Green policy, Green human sustainable resource management, Green technology are major drivers, Product flexibility and green supply chain management emerged as the most important enablers. Green policy and green supply chain management emerged as the most important linkages for sustainability strategy (findings from case studies).

- Although product flexibility doesn't affect sustainability directly, but it has indirect relation with the sustainability strategy.

- Our study suggest that orientation towards sustainability concept affects sustainability in different ways depending on whether people are allowed to adopt sustainable practices. Our study indicates that having defines objectives and a goal about sustaibility helps them to achieve the strategy better.

The above research findings, reflecting the achievement of research objectives to a great extent, led to the generation of some important recommendations, which have been partly tested in case studies.

9.3. IMPLICATIONS

9.3.1. Implications for Researchers

This research has several important implications. From a theoretical perspective, the current research provides an important empirical step towards understanding the internal drivers of sustainability. As previously noted, the literature in this area has been primarily normative in which most researchers have developed conceptual schema which requires empirical testing, or are based on limited case study analyses.

This study presents an empirical analysis that emphasizes the key internal drivers that are likely to impact corporate sustainable strategy. This focus clearly distinguishes this research from previous studies that tend to be concerned with more generalized assessments of organizations' readiness to initiate sustainability efforts.

The results can be used to steer further research in sustainability. The validated model includes management support, green human sustainable resource managementand work discretion. As compared to results published by Lai et al. (2010) and Mangal (2010), the findings of this study emphasizes on the importance of green technology and green policy as important predictors of sustainability which has not been included in earlier studies. Thus, the major writings in this area can therefore be used to guide further research into sustainability by focusing on the role of these factors uncovered in this study. These findings contribute to the theory of green policy proposed by Bhardwaj, Mangal, Lai (2012). Further research may be taken up to explore the relationship of this variable and the strategy of sustainability.

This study adds to the existing literature by identifying the role of green technology and green policy and highlight importance of future research with it. It is the perceptual aspect that may become most important for future research. The future research may include these factors to understand the influence of these two variables namely green technology, green human sustainable resource management, and green policy with sustainability strategy.

The results also indicate that before implementing any kind of change management initiatives including sustainable change, the organizations are likely to analyze the internal environment for stimulating such behavior. Further research efforts should aim at developing on this theory to measure the individual elements of green technology, green human sustainable resource management, product flexibility, green supply chain management and green policy and its relationship with sustainability strategy. Such a tool can be of prime importance to the organizations which can help the organizations to identify the elements to create appropriate environment for encouraging sustainable concept (Starik and Rands, 1995).

The case study results reveal that the structure, systems and sustainability vision play important role in implementing sustainability practice. Future researchers may focus on identifying the different types of structure which help to implement various practices of sustainability. Also the researchers may study the various systems which stimulate sustainability behavior within the organization. The future researchers may also study the impact of structure and systems on sustainability strategy.

9.3.2 Implications for Practitioners

The instrument developed in this study also has practical implications for managers. For example, the tool can be used as an assessment tool for evaluating corporate training requirements in sustainability and innovation. This kind of tool may further help the organizations to understand if they have the necessary internal environment to initiate sustainability. The results can help the organizations to identify the gaps. This tool can therefore be used as a diagnostic tool for sustainability. Many companies have initiated such programs in recent years to identify areas requiring attention to encourage sustainable concept. The results of one empirical analysis indicated that a training program designed to enhance sustainability significantly affected perceptions of the environment by managers (Bhardwaj et al., 2012). Therefore, the instrument developed in this study can be used as an investigative tool for identifying whether the organization has the necessary environment for initiating sustainability concept and the training needs to motivate the employees for sustainability. This research has also the practical implications in terms of managing change within the organization. The tool can be used to identify the preparedness of the organizations to adopt sustainable change. The present study also contributes towards the theory of sustainable revitalization of the organization to gain competitive advantage (Volberda, 1998).

The research findings related to organizational structure would help the managers to design proper structure for implementing sustainability. The various processes and systems which help to implementing sustainability would guide the mangers to design the right kind of systems which promote sustainability.

9.4.　MAJOR RECOMMENDATIONS

Findings of the questionnaire survey as well as case studies have been reflected upon and some major recommendations were generated in order to help the organizations understand the internal environmental factors necessary for stimulating sustainability strategy. The recommendations have emanated out of various components of research and are tagged with specific macro/micro variables and relevant research component.

- Designing right kind of organizational structure, processes, systems, and policy to implement sustainability.

- Introduction of an effective sustainable process is recommended in order to implement sustainability within organizations (Green policy – Green product development).

- Top management should dedicate reasonable time to work on imparting and communicating the green policy and sustainable strategy. Moreover, green adoption should also be encouraged within the organization facilitated by the top management and product flexibility. More emphasis on inter-departmental collaboration and cross functional teams should be there. The effort should be directed towards harnessing the collaborative expertise of the employees within the organization for developing sustainable solutions (Green policy – green human sustainable resource management – green product development).

- Green human sustainable resource management is necessary to enable movement of people and sustainable resources with the focus of optimum utilization of sustainable resources. This should be supported by management to make it more effective. Nevertheless, there should also be proper monitoring systems to control the sustainable resources allocated towards various sustainability concept. The employees could be made accountable towards their actions (Green technology adoption-sustainability strategy).

- It is recommended that the organization should have Management Support for implementing sustainability concept since it has emerged as a major driver, which acts as a pivot variable to influence the interrelationships between Green policy – green human sustainable resource management – green product development. These important inter relationships show that to have better sustainable strategy, management should support these concepts by providing organizational flexibility which can further stimulate adoption of sustainable practices.

- It is recommended that the organization should have proper organization structure and systems to facilitate the green policy, which has emerged as major driver of sustainability (Green policy - Sustainability Strategy).

- Due to its greater degree of technical, product, and market uncertainties, sustaibility efforts need, higher degree of cross functional coordination and a greater sense of urgency. The business unit organization structure is more costly due to duplication of sustainable resources, but better suited to sustainabilitythan either the functional or the matrix organization. Due to its dedicated cross-functional sustainable resources and clear accountability for results provide the required level of coordination, focus, and speed. In spite of this, its higher cost might not be suited for sustainable businesses.

- Although structural solutions are readily implemented, but it is best not to engage in a search for 'ideal' organization. In spite of availability of choices, the best results may be achieved by focusing on neglected task of developing the competencies of the people and capability to work within and across boundaries through proper education, training, coaching, and mentoring.

- The organization will do better if it focuses on creating conditions that encourage competent and committed people to volunteer to lead sustainability initiatives. These volunteers should be allowed to recruit other believers who have the necessary skills, and the team must have sufficient autonomy and sustainable resources to proceed.

- The other approach which works best in such situations include offering plenty of recognition and career advancement as reward, and reduce the perception of personal risk for stimulating the adoption of sustainable practices.

- The organization must provide sufficient sustainable resources and autonomy to decide which sustainable practices to take and how quickly to move within decided parameters.

9.5   SIGNIFICANT RESEARCH CONTRIBUTIONS

The study provided some new evidence on the relationship between sustainability and its antecedents. The analysis indicated that green policy (GP), green human sustainable resources management (GHRM) and green technology (GT) were some of the most important drivers of sustainability. The predictors of sustainability are green policy, management support and work discretion whereas the predictors of innovations include green policy, green human sustainable resource management and work discretion. This shows that for sustainability, it is important to have management support and proper processes for green policy. On the other hand, for innovations to succeed, it is important to have proper processes for green human sustainable resource management too. The study suggests that both sustainability and innovations require work discretion to succeed. However, the study suggests that it is more important for sustainability to be supported by management for the venture to succeed. This further validates the necessity of having proper processes for dissemination of information at all levels, emphasizes on having proper management support and work discretion for successful sustainability. The findings have contributed towards the existing theory of sustainability by extending the previous research (Starik and Rand, 1995). The positive nature of the relationship points out the fact that the employees should be given the autonomy in terms of abilities and selection of venture ideas for encouraging sustainability. Also, it is important to have management support in terms of financial support for sustainability concept.

The highly competitive and sustainable environment prevalent in most sectors is forcing many companies to adopt a sustainable strategy, which is seeking competitive advantage through innovation on a sustained basis. The current debate is more on 'how' of sustainability and the present study suggest some of the critical routes to follow. This requires the top management team to create an organizational setting that focuses the attention of individual participants on innovation as an important and expected activity and enables and directs group and firm behaviors towards sustainable ends. The team will also use appropriate processes to capture knowledge created in the innovation process and operate in a manner that enables integration of knowledge. Institutionalizing elements of sustainability is crucial for sustaining competitive organizations (Bhardwaj et al., 2013).

The significant research contributions with respect to sustainability strategy are discussed as follows:

- In order to investigate the internal organizational factors that encourage sustainability, an empirical analysis has been conducted.

- Case studies on four organizations have been carried out in detail. The roles of structures and systems have been studied through Sustainable SAP-LAP framework in the context of sustainability Strategy.

- The learnings from the questionnaire survey study and the case studies have been synthesized where a number of important findings have been reported, which provide a guiding framework for implementation of sustainability approach.

- A 'Sustainability Model' has been evolved, which may be used as guiding framework by the firms and managers intending to use the sustainability approach.

- Inter-strategy influence relationships have been identified and complementary nature of certain firm level macro strategies has been established. This would guide the managers in evolving and properly implementing the sustainability strategies at firm level.

- This study adds to the literature on sustainability by recording the existence of an underlying set of organizational factors that should be recognized in promoting sustainable concept within an organization. The five factors identified by Lai et al. (2010) through value chain analysis and natural sustainable resource based view (NRBV) were green policy, green human sustainable resource management and green technology which represent a parsimonious description of the internal organizational factors that influence sustainable activity within companies. These three factors accounted for 46 per cent variance in the corporate sustainable concept (Bhardwaj et al., 2012). The inclusion of two factors, i.e. product flexibility and green supply chain management explained the variance of 76 per cent (Bhardwaj et al., 2013).

- The current research provides an important empirical step towards understanding the internal factors that stimulate sustainability. As previously noted, the literature in this area has been primarily normative. This study presents an empirical analysis that emphasizes the key internal factors that impact corporate sustainable strategy. This focus clearly distinguishes this research from previous studies that tend to be concerned with more generalized assessments of organizations' readiness to initiate sustainability efforts.

- This highlights the importance of future research with the sustainability instrument. It is the perceptual aspect that may become most important for future research. The instrument developed in this study also has practical implications for managers. For example, the modified tool can be used as an assessment tool for evaluating corporate training requirements in sustainability and innovation. Many companies have initiated such programs in recent years to identify areas needing attention to encourage sustainability concept (Mangal, 2010). The results of one empirical analysis indicate that a training program designed to enhance sustainability appreciably affects perceptions of the environment by managers. Therefore, the instrument developed in this study can be used as an investigative tool for identifying whether the organization has the necessary environment for initiating sustainability concept and the training needs to motivate the employees for sustainability.

9.6   LIMITATIONS OF THE STUDY

The limitations of the study are given as follows:

- Strict random sampling has not been used for the questionnaire study. Further, purposive sampling has been used for the pilot study and case studies.

- Questionnaire design and data collection is based on the assumption that various sustainability strategies can be formulated and implemented in stand-alone manner. However, the research findings have brought out that various sustainability strategies are complementary and presence of critical organizational drivers are important for sustainability Strategy. The results also establish the inter relationship.

- More number of case studies in these two sectors can be undertaken to understand the impact of these organizational antecedents in wider aspects. The variables such as product flexibility and rewards can be studied in details in future research. Moreover, the role of green policy and Green human sustainable resource management can be explored further.

- As most of the organizations were not willing to disclose the actual quantified data relating to the specific sustainability concept in terms of total number of products/services/markets identified, the sustainability Strategy has been measured in qualitative terms through sustainability Strategy in comparison with likely Strategy of sustainability approach where these internal variables are not available.

- The external environmental factors such as technological dynamism and market potential have not been included in the empirical study.

- Corporate level strategies can be taken up for further research, which has not been included in this model.

9.7   STUDY IS RELEVANT TO WHOM

The study is relevant in the following ways:

- Business organizations that intend to implement or adopt sustainability approach. The 'Sustainability Model', which has been evolved in this research, can serve as guiding framework for implementing the sustainability strategy. The inter relationships explained through interpretive matrix can be useful in understanding the impact on sustainability strategy. This interpretive matrix may also be useful in understanding the various processes for implementing sustainability within the organization.

- Researchers and academicians pursuing sustainability research. The results can be used to steer further research into sustainability concept.

9.8   SUGGESTIONS FOR FURTHER WORK

The suggestions for future work are given below:

- An empirical study may be carried out taking into account the inter-strategy influence relationships and requirements of inter-strategy support, as brought out in this study.

- Study on sustainability approach may be carried in select organizations that may be willing to share actual quantified data in terms of sustainability strategy.

- A study may be made covering numbers of firms/organizations from USA, Europe, Japan and India to bring out the unique firm level sustainability practices pertaining to internal organizational drivers of sustainability strategy in various countries in view of differences in work culture and management systems/practices.

- Further research can be taken up by examining appropriate rewards and incentives, time available for employees to experiment and innovate, and the level of organizational support, researchers will be able to more clearly measure factors that influence employees' sustainability efforts.

- Further research efforts into corporate sustainable environments need to give special attention to the eight internal factors uncovered in this study, especially, the role of green policy and green human sustainable resource management in stimulating sustainability strategy.

- Future research can also incorporate external environment as a major variable to understand its impact on sustainability concept within the organizations.

- Moreover, the corporate level strategies including the vision for sustainability and leadership can also be an important contribution towards sustainability research.

The areas for additional research are proposed, corresponding roughly to the antecedents and strategy portions, respectively, of the model. Further research is needed to clarify the linkage between the presence of specific qualities or properties in an organizational context and individuals' (such as middle-level managers) decisions to act sustainably. Important contributions in this area have emerged from the research of Shrivastava (1995), Zangwill and Kantor (1998), and others, yet significant research questions remain. Moreover, these strategy are merely illustrative of the type of effects possibly resulting from sustainable behavior. A relatively small percentage of corporations can accurately claim to exhibit extensive sustainable activity within the ranks of their members. While past research on specific elements of the proposed model has demonstrated some significant relationships (i.e., organizational antecedents and self-reported strategy), additional research should be conducted to further delineate the roles of all managerial levels in the corporate sustainable process.

While this study suggests the existence of a set of factors necessary for new business creation, additional research addressing the relationship to such measures as the number of ideas generated in an organization; time spent on sustainable ideas; and employee willingness to break through organizational boundaries. Second, while this study has initiated an important exploration, clarification, and refinement of these factors, it is necessary to further support the relationship between the measures of individual new business concept. For example, researchers may link this framework's three dimensions to financial measures of organizational performance. While companies initiate sustainability efforts for varying reasons, ultimately, senior management expects sustainability efforts to improve the company's financial position. Consequently, future researchers could study the relationship between sustainability dimensions and financial performance measures. Finally, additional research into whether or not such variables as sector type and culture play a role in the corporate sustainable drivers is necessary. In summary, this study provides empirical evidence regarding the existence of internal drivers believed to enhance sustainability within the manufacturing and service sectors. The study's results and proposed framework offer a foundation for developing a reliable and valid measure of the firm's internal drivers for sustainability for manufacturing and services sectors.

9.9. CONCLUDING REMARKS

The main objective of this study was to study the key internal organizational factors that stimulate sustainability and develop a tool that measures these factors. To accomplish this purpose, the study collected data from 281 managers in 39 organizations. Results from the study can, thus, help to define internal organizational factors zone of influence and set the stage for better environment to enhance sustainable concept. The role of organizational factors for stimulating sustainability has been discussed. After identifying different organizational factors from literature, a discussion has been followed by an empirical study conducted to identify these key internal organizational factors. The results of the study and their implications for research and managerial practice have been discussed in detail.

This study has established that in the context of the fast changing needs of the customers, the adoption of sustainability is very important. The presence of internal organizational drivers/factors is critical for sustainability strategy. A sustainability model has been evolved, which may be used by organizations to assess the presence of necessary and critical internal factors for stimulating sustainability concept within the organization. This framework can further be enriched by subsequent studies.

References

ABB, Annual Business Report, The 37th Business Term, 2012, 5-12.

Adrian Henriques, Julie Richardson (2012) The Triple Bottom Line: Does It All Add Up, Earthscan publishers, London.

Ahuja, G. and Lampert, C. M. (2001) Sustainability in Large Corporation: A Longitudinal Study of How Established Firms Create Breakthrough Inventions, *Strategic Management Journal*, June-July Special Issue, 22, 521-543.

Amabile, T. M. (1998). A Model of Creativity in Organizations, Research in Organizational Behavior, 10, 123-168.

Arrow, K. J. (1980). Organizational Structure and Sustainable Concept, *The Entrepreneur's Role in Today's Society*, New York: Price Institute of Sustainable Studies.

Bandura, A. (1986) The Social Foundations of Thought and Action, Engelwood Cliffs, NJ: Prentice-Hall.

Barringer, B. R. and Bluedorn, A. C. (1999). The Relationship between Sustainability and Strategic Management, *Strategic Management Journal*, 20, 412-444.

Bhardwaj B.R., Sushil and Momaya K. (2007) Corporate entrepreneurship: Application of Moderator Method, *Singapore Management Review,* 29(1), First half 2007.

Brazeal D.V. (1993) Organizing for Internally Developed Corporate Ventures, *J. Bus. Venturing,* 8, 75-90.

Burgelman R.A. (1983a) A Process Model of Internal Corporate Venturing in the Diversified Major Firm, *Adm. Sci. Q.*, 28, 223-244.

Burgelman R.A. (1983b) Sustainability and Strategic Management: Insights from a Process Study, *Manage. Sci.,* 29, 1349-1363 (December).

Burgelman, R.A. (1983c) Sustainability and Strategic Management: Insights from a Process Study, *Management Science*, 29: 1349-1364.

Burgelman R.A. (1984a) Designs for Sustainability, *California Management Review*, 26, 154-166.

Burgelman R.A. (1984b) Managing the Internal Corporate Venturing Process, *Sloan Management Review*, 25(2), 33-48.

Burgelman, R.A. (1985) Managing the New Venture Division: Research Findings and Implications for Strategic Management, *Strategic Management Journal*, 6, 39-54.

Burgelman R.A. and Sayles L.R. (1986) Inside Corporate Innovation: Strategy, Structure, and Managerial Skills, Free Press, New York, NY.

Burgelman, R.A. (1988). Strategy making as a Social Learning Process: The Case of Internal Corporate Venturing, *Interfaces*, 18(3), pp-74-85.

Burgelman, R.A. (1996) A Process Model of Strategic Business Exit: Implications of Evolutionary Perspective on Strategy, *Strategic Management Journal*, Summer Special Issue, 17, 193-214.

Burgelman, R.A., and Doz, Y. L. (2001) The Power of Strategic Integration, *MIT Sloan Management Review*, 42(3), 28-38.

Burgelman, R.A. (2005) Managing Internal Corporate Venturing, *MIT Sloan Management Review*, Vol. 46(4), 26-34.

Barney, J. (1991) "Firm Sustainable resources and Sustained Competitive Advantage," *Journal of Management*, 17/1 (March 1991): 99-120.

Bhardwaj, B.R., Mangal, V. (Ann) and Lai, Kee-hung (2013) Impact of Green Policy on Ecologically Sustainable Organization: A Study in Emerging Market Context, Accepted for publication in International Journal of Global Business Competitiveness, 2013.

Bhardwaj, B.R., Sushil, (2012) Corporate Entrepreneurship: Assessing CEAI
    Scale for Emerging Markets, *Journal of Chinese Entrepreneurship*, 4(1), 70-89.

Bhatnagar, Ashima, Bhardwaj, B.R., Gupta, Shikha, (2012) Challenges faced by Women Entrepreneurs, 'Opinion'- International Journal of Business Management.

Brundtland, H.G. (1987) World Commission on Environment and development.

Bhardwaj, B.R., Sushil, Momaya, K. (2011) Encouraging Corporate Entrepreneurship:
    The Transformation of India's XYZ, *Strategic Direction*, 27 (6), 19-21.

Burnett, D.R. and Hansen, D.R. (208) Ecoefficiency: Defining a Role for Environmental Cost Management, *Accounting ,Organizations and Society*, 33/6 (August 2008): 551-581.

Bhardwaj, B.R., Sushil, Momaya, K. (2011) Case Studies of Social
    Entrepreneurship in Indian Context: SAP-LAP Learning Critical Success Factors, *International Journal of Economics Management and Engineering* (IJEME), Volume 2 - Issue 2/3, pp. 231 – 251.

D'Souza C, Taghian M, Lamb P, Peretiatkos R (2006). Green products and corporate strategy: an empirical investigation. Soc. Bus. Rev., 1(2): 144-157.

Das Gandhi NM, Selladurai V, Santhi P (2006). Green productivity indexing A practical step towards integrating environmental protection into corporate performance. Int. J. Prod. Perform. Manag., 55(7):594-606.

Dougherty, D. and Bowman, E. H. (1995) The Effects of Downsizing on Product Innovation, *California Management Review*, 37(4), 28-44.

Drucker, P. F. (1954) The Practice of Management, New York: Harper and Row.

Floortje Blindenbach-Driessen, Jan Van Dalen, and Jan Van Den Ende (2010) Subjective Performance Assessment of Innovation Projects, Journal of Product Innovation Management, Volume 27, Issue 4, pages 572–592, July 2010.

Hart, S.L. "A Natural-Sustainable resource-Based View of the Firm," *The Academy of Management Review*, 20/4 (October 1995): 986-1014.

Graham, Michael (2006) Al Gore's Force of Nature, www.discoverthenetworks.org/individualProfile.

Hart (1995), op. cit.; M.A. Berry and D.A. Rondinelli, "Proactive Corporate Environmental Management: A New Industrial Revolution," *Academy of Management Executive*, 12/2 (May 1998): 38-50.

M & M, Corporate Governance Update, 2012.

Elkington, John and Hartigan, Pamela (2008) *The Power of Unreasonable People: How Social Entrepreneurs Create Markets That Change the World*, Harvard Business School Press.

Mangal, Vandana Ann. (2010). Sustainability - is it for the CIO?. Electronic Green Journal, 1(29). Retrieved from: http://escholarship.org/uc/item/0rp658mr

Orlitzky, Marc, Siegel, Donald S. and Waldman, David A. (2011) Strategic Corporate Social Responsibility and Environmental Sustainability, Business Society March 2011 vol. 50 no. 1 6-27.

Shrivastava, P., "The Role of Corporations in Achieving Ecological Sustainability," *The Academy of Management Review*, 20/4 (October 1995): 936-960.

Melville, Nigel P. (2010) Information Systems Innovation For Environmental Sustainability, MIS Quarterly, 34(1), 1-21.

Gonzalez-Benito, J. (2008) The effect of manufacturing pro-activity on environmental management: an exploratory analysis. International Journal of Production Research, 46(24), 7017-7038.

Sarkis, Joseph; Zhu, Qinghua; Lai, Kee-hung (2011) An organizational theoretic review of green supply chain management literature, International Journal of Production Economics, 130(1), 1-15.

Lam, Patrick T. I.; Chan, Edwin H. W.; Chau, C. K.; Poon, C. S. (2011) A sustainable framework of "green" specification for construction in Hong Kong, Journal of Facilities Management, 9(1), 16-33.

Klassen, Robert D.; Biehl, Markus (2009) Toward Assessing Financial Returns From Green Structural and Infrastructural Expenditures, Academy of Management Annual Meeting Proceedings, 1-6.

O'sullivan and Shefrin (2002) Journal of Sustainable Development , 2: 156–8.

Drucker, P. F. (1985a) *Innovation and Sustainability: Principles and Practice*, New York: Harper and Row.

Eisenhartdt K.M. and Tabrizi B.N. (1995) Accelerating Adaptive Processes: Product Innovation in the Global Computer Sector, *Academy Management Journal,* 32(3), 543-576.

Floyd S.W. and Lane P.J. (2000) Strategizing throughout the Organization: Managing Role Conflict in Strategic Renewal, *Academy of Management Review*, 25, 154–177.

Floyd S.W. and Woolridge B. (1990) The Strategy Process, Middle Management Involvement, and Organizational Performance, *Strategic Manage. J.,* 13, 53-242.

Floyd S.W. and Woolridge B. (1992) Middle Management Involvement in Strategy and its Association with Strategic Role Type: A Research Note, *Strategic Manage. J.,* 3(34), 465-485 (May).

Freidman, T. (2000) The Lexus and the Olive Tree, Published by Anchor Books, USA.

Ginsberg A. and Hay M. (1994) Confronting the Challenges of Sustainability: Guidelines for Venture Managers, *Eur. Manage. J.*, 12, 82-389.

Graham P. (1995) *Mary Parker Follet - Prophet of Management,* Boston: Harvard Business School Press.

Haddad C.J. (1996) Operationalising the Concept of Concurrent Engineering: A Case Study from the US Auto Sector, *IEEE Transactions on Engineering Management,* 43(2), May, 124-132.

Hair, J.F., Anderson, R. E, Tatham R. L. and Black, W.C. (1998) *Multivariate Data Analysis*, 5th Edition, Pearson Education.

Hambrick, D. C. (1987) The Top Management Team: Key to Strategic Success, *California Management Review*, 30(1), 88-108.

Charantimath, P.M. (2006) Entrepreneurship Development and Small Business Enterprise. Author, Edition, reprint. Publisher, Pearson Education India.

Desai, S. (forthcoming) "Entrepreneurship and a Tale of Two Cities," Journal of Small Business and Entrepreneurship, 2013.

TH Chiles, AC Bluedorn, VK Gupta (2007) Beyond creative destruction and entrepreneurial discovery: a radical Austrian approach to entrepreneurship, Organization Studies, 28(04): 467–493, ISSN 0170–8406

GA Zsidisin, SP Siferd (2001) Environmental purchasing: a framework for theory development, European Journal of Purchasing & Supply Management, Volume 7, Issue 1, March 2001, Pages 61–73.

Joseph Raymond Huscroft, Jr. (2010) The Reverse Logistics Process in the Supply Chain and Managing Its Implementation, Ph.D. book submitted to Auburn, Alabama University.

Qinghua Zhu, Joseph Sarkis and Kee-hung Lai (2008) Confirmation of a measurement model for green supply chain management practices implementation, International Journal of Production Economics, Volume 111, Issue 2, February 2008, Pages 261–273

Samir K. Srivastava (2007) Green supply-chain management: A state-of the-art literature review, *International Journal of Management Reviews (2007);* doi: 10.1111/j.1468-2370.2007.00202.x

Cater, C.R. and Jnnings M.M. (2002) Social responsibilities, and supply chain management, Transportation Resarch, Part E 38, 37-52.

Ginovsky, John, 2009. Green banking. Community Banker; Apr2009, Vol. 18 Issue 4, p30-32, 3p.

Hemantkumar P. Bulsara, Shailesh Gandhi & P. D. Porey, *Techno-innovation to Techno –Entrepreneurship through Technology Business Incubation in India: An Exploratory Study,* Asia Pacific Journal of Innovations and Entrepreneurship, Asian Association of Business Incubation, Vol.3, No.1, May, 2009, pp 55 – 77.

Kee-hung Lai, T.C.E. Cheng, Ailie K.Y. Tang (2010) Green Retailing: factors for success, California Management Review, Vol. 52, No. 2, pg-6-31.

Reinhardt, F. L. *Down to Earth: Applying Business Principles to Environmental Management.* Boston: Harvard Business School Press, 2000.

Pravakar Sahoo, Bibhu Prasad Nayak, 2008. Green banking in India. *Indian Economic Journal (IE), paper series no.125/2008.*

Jeucken, M and Bouma, J,J (1999) "The Changing Environment of Banks" GMI Theme Issue, GMI-27, Autumn, 1999.

Rutherford, Michael (1994),*"At what Point can pollution be said to cause damage to the Environment?"*, *The Banker*, January.

Schmidheiny, S and Federico J L Zorraquin, (1996), *"Financing Change: The Financial Community, Eco-Efficiency and Sustainable development"*, Cambridge, MIT Press.

Gupta, S, (2003), *"Do Stock market penalise Environment-Unfriendly Behaviour? Evidence from India"*, Delhi School of Economics working Paper Series, No-116.

Ellis, BillieJ, Jr Sharon S Willians and Sandra Y Bodeau, (1992), *"Helping a Lender Develop Environmental Risk Program,"* The Practical Real Estate Layer, July.

Jeucken, M and Bouma, J,J (1999) "The Changing Environment of Banks" GMI Theme Issue, GMI-27, Autumn, 1999.

Blacconiere, Walter and Dennis Pattern, (1993), *"Environment Disclosure, regulatory costs and changes in firm values,"* Journal of Accounting and Economics (December).

Hamilton, James T (1995), "Pollution as News: Media and Stock markets Reactions to the toxics release inventory data", *Journal of Environmental Economics and management* 28.

Hall, Jeremy K., Daneke, Gregory A,Lenox, Michael J, 2010. *Sustainable development and entrepreneurship: past contributions and future directions.* Journal of Business Venturing; Sep2010, Vol. 25 Issue 5, p439-448, 10p.

Douglas J. Lober, (1998) "Pollution prevention as corporate entrepreneurship", Journal of Organizational Change Management, Vol. 11 Iss: 1, pp.26 – 37

Pacheco, Desirée F, Dean, Thomas J and Payne, David S (2010). "Escaping the green prison: Entrepreneurship and the creation of opportunities for sustainable development." Journal of Business Venturing; Sep2010, Vol. 25 Issue 5, p464-480, 17p.

Boks C (2006). The soft side of ecodesign. J. Clean. Prod., 14: 1346-1356.

Chan RY (2001). Determinants of Chinese consumers – green purchase behaviour. Psychol. Market. 18(4): 389-413.

Chang NJ, Fong CM (2010). Green product quality, green corporate image, green customer satisfaction, and green customer loyalty. Afr. J. Bus. Manage. 4(13): 2836-2844.

D'Souza C, Taghian M, Lamb P, Peretiatkos R (2006). Green products and corporate strategy: an empirical investigation. Soc. Bus. Rev., 1(2): 144-157.

Lubin, David A.; Esty, Daniel C. (2010) The Sustainability Imperative, Harvard Business Review, Vol. 88 Issue 5, p42-50.

Vitola, Alise; Senfelde, Maija (2010) The optimization of national development planning system as a precondition for competitiveness and sustainability of national economy, Economics & Management, p325-331.

Hart SL (2005). Innovation, creative destruction and sustainability, Res. Technol. Manage., 48(5): 21-7.

Pujari D, Peattie K, Wright G (2004). Organizational antecedents of environmental responsiveness in industrial new product development. Ind. Mark. Manag. 33: 381–391.

Saxena AK, Bhardwaj KD, Sinha KK (2003). Sustainable growth through green productivity: a case of edible oil industry in India. Int. Energy J., 4(1): 81-91.

Ritzén S (2000) Integrating Environmental Aspects into Product Development – Proactive Measures. PhD Book. Department of Machine Design. Royal Institute of Technology. Stockholm.

Khandwalla PN, Mehta K (2004). Design of corporate creativity. J. Decis. Makers Vikalpa. 29(1): 13-28.

Teece, D. (1987) *Profiting from Technological Innovation: Implications for Integration, Collaboration, Licensing, and Public Policy. The Competitive Challenge* (Cambridge, MA:Ballinger.

Hong IH, Ammons JC, Realff MJ (2008). Decentralized decision-making and protocol design for recycled material flows. Int. J. Prod. Econ., 116: 325–337.

198

Ehrenfeld J, Lenox M (1997). The Development and Implementation of DfE Programmes. J. Sustain. Prod. Des., 1: 17-27.

Gou Q, Liang L, Huang Z, Xu C. (2008). A joint inventory model for an open-loop reverse supply chain. Int. J. Prod. Econ., 116: 28–42.

Douglas J. Lober, (1998) "Pollution prevention as corporate entrepreneurship", Journal of Organizational Change Management, Vol. 11 Iss: 1, pp.26 – 37

Pacheco, Desirée F, Dean, Thomas J and Payne, David S (2010). "Escaping the green prison: Entrepreneurship and the creation of opportunities for sustainable development." Journal of Business Venturing; Sep2010, Vol. 25 Issue 5, p464-480, 17p.

Chan RY (2001). Determinants of Chinese consumers – green purchase behaviour. Psychol. Market. 18(4): 389-413.

Fitzgerald K (1993). It's green, it's friendly, it's wal-mart, eco-store. Advert. Age, 1: 44.

Kumar S, Putnam V (2008). Cradle to cradle: reverse logistics strategies and opportunities across three industry sectors. Int. J. Prod. Econ., 115: 305–31

Xu Feng Ju; Mirza, Sultan Sikandar (2012) Chinese Competitiveness and Growth Sustainability, _ International Journal of Business & Social Science, Vol. 3 Issue 3, p69-73.

Saxena AK, Bhardwaj KD, Sinha KK (2003). Sustainable growth through green productivity: a case of edible oil industry in India. Int. Energy J., 4(1): 81-91.

Ehrenfeld J, Lenox M (1997). The Development and Implementation of DfE Programmes. J. Sustain. Prod. Des., 1: 17-27.

Salvati, Luca; Carlucci, Margherita (2011) The economic and environmental performances of rural districts in Italy: Are competitiveness and sustainability compatible targets? Ecological Economics, Vol. 70 Issue 12, p2446-2453.

Schuller, Bernd-Joachim (2011) Swedish and Baltic competitiveness in a European perspective -- some quantitative aspects, Applied Economics: Systematic Research, Vol. 5 Issue 1, p63-76.

Peter Jones, Colin Clarke-Hill, Daphne Comfort, David Hillier, (2008) "Marketing and sustainability", Marketing Intelligence & Planning, Vol. 26 Iss: 2, pp.123 - 130

John, Stephen (2012) Implementing Sustainability Strategy: a Community Based Change Approach, International Journal of Business Insights & Transformation, Special Issue, Vol. 4, p16-20.

Lubin, David A.; Esty, Daniel C. (2010) The Sustainability Imperative, Harvard Business Review, Vol. 88 Issue 5, p42-50.

Bhardwaj, B.R., Jain, S.K., Ault, S. (2011) Impact of Intelligence Dissemination on New Business Creation, *Singapore Management Review*, 33(2), 2011.

Bhardwaj, B.R., Sushil, & K. Momaya (2011). Drivers and Enablers of Corporate Entrepreneurship: Case of a Software Giant from India. *Journal of Management Development*, 30(2):187 – 205.
Salvati, Luca; Carlucci, Margherita (2011) The economic and environmental performances of rural districts in Italy: Are competitiveness and sustainability compatible targets? Ecological Economics, Vol. 70 Issue 12, p2446-2453.

Hamel G. and Prahlad C.K. (1991) Corporate Imagination and Expeditionary Marketing, *Harvard Business Review*, July/August, 81-92.

Nidumolu, Ram; Prahalad, C. K.; Rangaswami, M. R. (2009) Why sustainability is now the key driver of innovation, Harvard Business Review, Vol. 87 Issue 9, p56-64.

Hamel, G. and Prahalad, C. K. (1994) *Competing for the Future*, Boston: Harvard Business School Press.
Hamel, G. (2006) Innovation Gap, *Leadership Excellence*, Vol. 23(12), 9-10.

Hamel, G. (2007) Management Innovation, *Leadership Excellence*, Vol. 24(1), 5-15.

Hisrich R. D. and Peters M.P. (1986) Establishing a New Business Venture Unit Within a Firm, J. *Bus. Venturing,* 1, 307-322.

Hisrich R. D. and Peters M.P. (1998) *Sustainability: Starting, Developing, and Managing a New Enterprise* (4th Ed.). Chicago: Irwin.

Hitt, M. A., Nixon, R., and Hoskisson, R., and Kochhar, R. (1999) Sustainability and Cross Fertilization, *Sustainability Theory and Practice*, 23(3), 145-167.

Ireland R.D., Hitt M.A., Camp S.M. and Sexton D.L. (2001) Integrating Sustainability Actions and Strategic Management Actions to Create Firm Wealth, Academy of Management Executive, 15(1), 95–106.

Ireland R.D., Hitt M.A. and Sirmon D.G. (2003) A Model of Strategic Sustainability, Journal of Management, 29, 963–989.

Judge, W. Q., Fryxell, G. E., and Dooley, R. S. (1997) The New Task of R&D Management: Creating Goal-directed Communities for Innovation, California Management Review, 39(3), 72-85.

Kanter, R. M. (1982) The Middle Managers as Innovators, *Harvard Business Review*, 60(4), 95-105.

Kanter, R. M. (1983) *The Change Masters*, New York: Simon and Schuster.

Kanter R.M. (1985) Supporting Innovation and Venture Development in Established Companies, *J. Bus. Venturing*, 1, 47-60.

Kanter, R. M. (1997). Frontiers of Management, Boston Mass: Harvard Business School Press.

Khandwalla P.N. (1974) Style of Management and Environment: Some Findings, *Academy of Management Proceedings*, 6-16.

Khandwalla P.N. (1974) Mass Output Orientation of Operations Technology and Organizational Structure, *Administrative Science Quarterly*, Vol. 19(1), 24-74.

Khandwalla P.N. (1977) *The Designs of Organizations*, New York: Harcourt Brace Jovanovich.

Khandwalla P.N. (1987) Generators of Pioneering-Innovative Management: Some Indian Evidence, Organization Studies, Vol. 8, No. 1, 39-59.

Khandwalla P.N. (1988) *Fourth Eye: Excellence through Creativity*, Allahabad: Wheeler Publications.

Khandwalla P.N. (2001) Role Sustainables among Industrial Entrepreneurs, Journal of Business Management, 2(1).

Khandwalla P.N. (2003) *Corporate Creativity – The Winning Edge*, New Delhi: Tata McGraw-Hill Publishing Company Ltd.

Khandwalla, P (2004a) *Lifelong Creativity: Unending Quest,* New Delhi: Tata McGraw-Hill.

Khandwalla P.N. (2004b) Design of Corporate Creativity, *Vikalpa*, 29(1), 13-28.

Khandwalla P.N. (2006) Tools for Enhancing Innovativeness in Enterprises, *Vikalpa*, 30(1), 1-16.

King A.W., Fowler, S.W. and Zeithaml C.P. (2001) Managing Organizational Competencies for Competitive Advantage: The Middle-management Edge, *Academy of Management Executive*, 15(2), 95–106.

Kogut, B. and Zander, U. (1992) Knowledge of the firm and the evolutionary theory of the multinational firm, Journal of International Business, Fourth quarter, 625-644.

Kirzner I. M. (1973) *Competition and Sustainability,* Chicago: University of Chicago Press.

Lorange, P. (1999) The Internal Entrepreneur as Driver of Growth, *General Management Review*, 1(1), 8-14.

Miller, D. (1983). The Correlates of Sustainability in Three Types of Firms. Management Science, 29, pp-770-791.

Miller D. and Friesen P.H. (1982) Innovation in Conservative and Sustainable Firms: Two Models of Strategic Momentum, *Strategic Management Journal*, 3, 1-25.

Miller, D. and Friesen, P. H. (1983) Strategy-making and Environment: The Third Link, Strategic Management Journal, 4, 221-235.

Oakey, R. P., (2003). Technical Entrepreneurship in High Technology Small Firms: Some Observations on the Implication for Management. *Technovation*, 23 (8), 679 – 688.

Kakati, M., (2003). Success Criteria in High Tech New Ventures. *Technovation*, 23,447-457.

Sung, T. K., Gibson, D.V., Kang B.S., (2003). Characteristics of Technology Transfer in Business Ventures: The Case of Daejon, Korea. *Technological Forecasting and Social Change,* 70, 449 – 466.

Routroy, Srikanta (2009) Antecedents and Drivers for Green Supply Chain Management Implementation in Manufacturing Environment. ICFAI Journal of Supply Chain Management, Mar2009, Vol. 6 Issue 1, p20-35

Craig R. Carter, P. Liane Easton, (2011) "Sustainable supply chain management: evolution and future directions", International Journal of Physical Distribution & Logistics Management, Vol. 41 Iss: 1, pp.46 - 62

Harvey, P. (2011) Sustainable Supply Chains for Rural Water Services: Linking local procurement of handpumps and spare parts supply. Field Note No 2011-1 Industrial Application Review for Sustainable Supply Chain Management, Mengxun NIE1,Yu XIONG2, Ying LIAO3 , *Journal of Cambridge Studies*, 15-25.

Trine-Lise Anker-Rasch and Siri Daviknes Sørgard (2011) Green Supply Chain Management : *A Study of Green Supply Chain Management within the pulp and paper industry,* Book submitted to Norwegian School Of Economics And Business Administration , 2011.

Charles O. Holliday, Jr., Stephan Schmidheiny, Philip Watts (2011) Walking the Talk: The Business Case for Sustainable Development, 2011.

Palanisamy R. (2001) Evolving Internet Business Model for Electronic Commerce using Flexible Systems Methodology, Global Journal of Flexible Systems Management, 2(3), 1-12.

Rosner, M. M. (1968) Administrative Controls and Innovation, Behavioral Science, 13, 36-43.

Saleh S.D. and Wang C.K. (1993) The Management of Innovation: Strategy, Structure and Organizational Climate, *IEEE Transactions on Engineering Management,* 40(1), 14-20.

Sathe V. (1985) Managing the Sustainable Dilemma: Nurturing Sustainability and Control in Large Organizations, *Frontiers of Sustainability Research*, 636-656.

Sathe V. (1989) Fostering Sustainability in Large Diversified Firm, *Organ. Dyn.,* 18, 20-32.

Sathe V. (2005) *Corporate entreprenweurship: Top Managers and New Business Creation,* Cambridge, MA: Harvard University Press.

Slater S.F. and Narver J.C. (1995) Market Orientation and the Learning Organization, *Journal of Marketing,* 59(3), 63-74.

Stajkovic A.D. and Luthans F. (2001) Differential Effects of Incentive Motivators on Work Performance, *Academy of Management Journal*, 44, 580–591.

Stevenson H.H. and Jarillo J.C. (1990) A Paradigm of Sustainability: Sustainable Management. *Strategic Management Journal*, 11, 17-27.

Stopford J.M. and Baden-Fuller C.W. (1994) Creating Sustainability, *Strategic Manage. J.,* 15, 521-536.

Stopford, J.M., and Baden-Fuller, C.W. (1990) Corporate Rejuvenation, *Journal of Management Studies*, 27(4), 399-415.

Stopford J.M. and Baden-Fuller C.W. (1994) Creating Sustainability, *Strategic Management Journal*, 15, 521-536.
Sushil (1993) Flexible Systems Approach to Management in Borderless World, *Proceedings of IEEE International Engineering Management Conference, New Delhi,* 207-211.

Sushil (1994) Flexible Systems Methodology, *System Practice,* 7(6), 633-652.

Sushil (1997) Flexible Systems Management: An Evolving Paradigm, *Systems Research & Behavioral Science*, 14(4), 259-275.

Sushil (1999) Sitution-Actor-Process Options: Mapping and Enhancing Flexibility, *System Research and Behavioral Science*, 16.

Sushil (2000) Concept of Systemic Flexibility, *Global Journal of Flexible Systems Management*, 1(1), 77-80.

Sushil (2001) Flexsy Tools, *Global Journal of Flexible Systems Management*, 2(3), 45-50.

Sushil (2005) Interpretive Matrix: A Tool to Aid Interpretation of Management and Social Research, *Global Institute of Flexible Systems Management*, (2), 27-30.

Sushil (2006) Leadership and Organizational Revitalization, in *Explorations in Management Thought* by Deepak Dogra and Vinay Auluck, 148-158, Ane Books India Publications.

Teece, D. J. (1987) Profiting from Technological Innovation: Implications for Integration, Collaboration, Licensing, and Public Policy, In D. J. Teece (ed.), The Competitive Challenge: Strategies for Industrial Innovation and Renewal, Cambridge, MA: Ballinger, 185-219.

Tettech E. and Burn J. (2001) Global Strategy for SME-Business: Applying the Small Framework, *Logistics Information Management*, 14 (1/2), 171-180.

Upton D.M. (1994) The Management of Manufacturing Flexibility, *California Management Review*, 36(2), 72-89.

Van de Ven, A. H. (1986). Central Problems in the Management of Innovation, Management Science, 3, 92-116.
Volberda H.H. (1998) *Building the Flexible Firm: How to Remain Competitive*, Oxford University Press.
Yin R.K. (1994) *Applications of Case Study Research*, Beverly Hills, CA: Sage Publishing.

Yin R.K. (2002) *Case Study Research: Design and Methods* (3rd Edition), Sage Publications, Thousand Oaks, CA.

Zhang, Linda L.; Xu, Qianli; Yu, Yugang; Jiao, Roger J. (2012) Domain-based production configuration with constraint satisfaction, *International Journal of Production Research*. Dec2012, Vol. 50 Issue 24, p7149-7166.

Starik, Mark and Rands, Gordon P. (1995) Weaving an Integrated Web: Multilevel and Multisystem Perspectives of Ecologically Sustainable Organizations, *The Academy of Management Review,* Vol. 20, No. 4 (Oct., 1995), pp. 908-935.

Zenger T.R. and Marshall C.R. (2000) Determinants of Incentive Intensity in Group-based Rewards, *Academy of Management Journal,* 43(2), 149–164.

APPENDICES

APPENDIX I

Definitions of Variables for the Study

Green Policy: It is defined as the design of vision, mission and objectives including the sustainability parameters and sustainability strategy.

Green Human Sustainable resource Management: It is defined as the orientation of employees to facilitate and promote sustainable behavior; including the championing of innovative ideas and providing financial sustainable resources required for sustainable actions.

Product Flexibility: The degree of flexibility in terms of designing green products and inter-departmental movements of sustainable resources for sustainable concept.

Green technology: Defined as the degree of development or acquisition of green sustainable technology for reducing emission and increasing recycling.

Green supply chain management: Collaborating with various stakeholders including the suppliers for designing the sustainable transportation system for reducing the carbon footprints and to ensure that individuals and groups have the time needed to pursue sustainable innovations.

Sustainability: Defined as proactive behavior through which organizations seek several strategy such as recycling, reducing the carbon emission, of innovation and sustainable renewal.

QUESTIONNAIRE FOR THE SURVEY STUDY

Bharati Vidyapeeth University, Delhi

Department of Management Studies

Hauz Khas, New Delhi – 110016

25th March 2005

Dear

I am pursuing Ph.D research programme at Department of Management Studies, IIT Delhi under the guidance of Prof. Sushil and Dr. K. Momaya, on "Internal Environment for Sustainability: A Study of Select Organizations" in the Indian context.

With a view to collect research data for my study, I seek your views as sustainability expert working in the country, as per the questionnaire enclosed.

There are sixty questions in all measuring different organizational antecedents for sustainability. Kindly answer the questions keeping your organization in mind.

For each questions there are six reply options indicated in the blocks on a scale of one to six where "1=Strongly Disagree" and "6=Strongly Agree".

May I request you to kindly return the questionnaire at the earliest possible. A self-addressed stamped envelope is also enclosed for your convenience.

With regards,

Dr./Shri/Smt. ……………………..   Your's sincerely,

………………………………………   (Broto Rauth Bhardwaj)

Name of respondent _____

Designation _____

Age _____ year(s)

Gender   F ☐   M ☐

Experience in current organization _____ year(s)

Total experience _____ year(s)

	1	2	3	4	5		1	2	3	4	5
We value the orderly and risk-reducing management process much more highly than leadership initiatives for product development.						I clearly know what level of work performance is expected from me in terms of amount, quality, time, and timeliness of output.					
Top managers in this business unit like to "play it safe".						We have rigid administrative processes and strictly adhere to bureaucratic practices.					
Top managers around like to implement ideas only if they are certain that the products developed will do well in the market.						We have good communication and free flow of information throughout the organization.					
Employees are not penalized for taking risk.						We poll end users at least once a year to assess the quality of our products and services.					
Risk-taking is considered a positive trait in the company.						In our business unit, intelligence on our competitors is generated independently by several departments.					
The organization tolerates failure.						We periodically review the likely effect of changes in our business environment (e.g. regulation) on customers.					

A 5

	1	2	3	4	5		1	2	3	4	5
Upper management is aware and very receptive to my ideas and suggestions.						In this business unit, we frequently collect and evaluate general macroeconomic information (e.g. interest rate, exchange rate, gross domestic product, sector growth rate, inflation rate).					
Promotion usually follows the development of new and innovative ideas.						In this business unit, we maintain contacts with officials of government & regulatory bodies (e.g. Department of Agriculture, Food and Drug Administration, Federal Trade Commission, Congress) in order to collect and evaluate the pertinent information.					
The employees who come up with innovative ideas on their own often receive management encouragement.						In this business unit, we collect and evaluate information concerning general social trends (e.g. environmental consciousness, emerging lifestyles) that might affect our business.					
	1	2	3	4	5		1	2	3	4	5
Money is often available to get new product ideas of the ground.						In this business unit, we spend time with our suppliers to learn more about various aspects of their business (e.g. manufacturing process, sector practices, and clientele).					
Individuals with successful innovative products receive additional reward and compensation for their ideas.						In this business unit, only a few people are collecting competitor information.					
This organization supports many small and experimental product developments realizing that some will eventually fail.						Marketing personnel in our business unit spend time discussing customers' future needs with other functional departments.					
A worker with a good idea is often given free time to develop that idea into product.						Our business unit periodically circulates documents (e.g. reports, newsletters) that provide information on our customers.					
I feel that I am my own boss and do not have to double-check all of my decisions.						We have cross-functional meetings very often to discuss market trends and developments (e.g.					

A 6

				customers, competition, and suppliers).				
This organization provides the chance to be creative and try my own methods of doing the job.				We regularly have interdepartmental meetings to update our knowledge of regulatory requirements.				
This organization provides freedom to use my own judgment.				Technical people in this business unit spend a lot of time-sharing information about technology for new products with other departments.				
This organization provides the chance to do something that makes use of my abilities.				Market information spreads quickly through all levels in this business unit.				
The selection of new business is done in a very systematic way.				During the past three months, my workload was too heavy to spend time on developing new ideas.				
I have the freedom to decide what I do on my job.				I always seem to have plenty of time to get everything done.				
I have autonomy on my job and am left on my own to do my own work.				I have just the right amount of time and workload to do everything well.				
The rewards I receive are dependent upon my work on the job.				My job is structured so that I have very little time to think about wider organizational problems.				
Special recognition is given if my work performance is especially good.				I feel that I am always working with time constraint on my job.				
My manager would tell his boss if my work was outstanding.				My co-workers and I always find time for long-term problem solving.				
My supervisor will increase my job responsibilities if I am performing well in my job.				In the past few years, the number of products developed have increased.				
Good ideas are given appropriate rewards.				In the past few years, the number of services provided to the customers have increased.				

My manager helps me get my work done by removing obstacles.					In the past few years, the number of markets where our products are being sold have increased.				

	1	2	3	4	5	6		1	2	3	4	5	6
In the past three months, I have always followed standard operating procedures or practices to do my major tasks.							In the past few years, the number of ideas generated for product development have increased.						
There are many written rules and procedures that exist for doing my major tasks.							In the past few years, the number of ideas for product improvement (new feature to existing product) have increased.						
During the past year, my immediate supervisor discussed my work performance with me frequently.							We value and encourage the new ideas within the organization.						
My job description clearly specifies the standards of performance on which my job is evaluated.							We value the market innovations within the organization.						

APPENDIX III

Regression Analysis

EFFECT OF GREEN TECHNOLOGY, POLICIES AND ECO ADVERTISING ON CUSTOMER PREFERENCE

Table 5.5(b): ANOVA Summary for Sustainability as Dependent Variable (Macro Variables)

Model		Sum of Squares	df	Mean Square	F	Sig.
1	Regression	47.136	8	5.892	5.052	.000(a)
	Residual	38.484	33	1.166		
	Total	85.619	41			

a Predictors: (Constant), enhance water and energy conservation, environmental arguments in marketing, Explicit definition of environmental policy, emission filters and end-of-pipe control, acquisition of clean technology/equipment, reduces green house gas emission, green packaging, clear objectives and long term environmental plans
b Dependent Variable: preference for green products in purchasing

Coefficients(a)

Model		Unstandardized Coefficients		Standardized Coefficients		
		B	Std. Error	Beta	t	Sig.
1	(Constant)	-.659	1.025		-.643	.525
	Explicit definition of environmental policy	.515	.254	.304	2.026	.051
	clear objectives and long term environmental plans	.781	.309	.604	2.528	.016
	environmental arguments in marketing	.063	.146	.063	.430	.670
	green packaging	-.871	.300	-.574	-2.905	.007
	acquisition of clean technology/equipment	-.172	.242	-.112	-.710	.483
	reduces green house gas emission	-.133	.182	-.132	-.734	.468
	emission filters and end-of-pipe control	-.044	.173	-.037	-.256	.800
	enhance water and energy conservation	.687	.280	.455	2.456	.019

a Dependent Variable: preference for green products in purchasing

b) EFFECT OF POLICIES AND MANAGEMENT SUPPORT ON GMP CONTROL PROCEDURE

ANOVA(b)

Model		Sum of Squares	df	Mean Square	F	Sig.
1	Regression	24.083	4	6.021	8.007	.000(a)
	Residual	27.822	37	.752		
	Total	51.905	41			

a Predictors: (Constant), full-time employees devoted to environmental management, Explicit definition of environmental policy, well-defined environmental responsibilities, clear objectives and long term environmental plans
b Dependent Variable: periodic elaboration of environmental reports

Coefficients(a)

Model		Unstandardized Coefficients		Standardized Coefficients	t	Sig.
		B	Std. Error	Beta		
1	(Constant)	.514	.808		.637	.528
	Explicit definition of environmental policy	-.083	.187	-.063	-.443	.660
	clear objectives and long term environmental plans	-.024	.189	-.024	-.126	.900
	well-defined environmental responsibilities	.173	.173	.165	.999	.324
	full-time employees devoted to environmental management	.463	.091	.686	5.076	.000

a Dependent Variable: periodic elaboration of environmental reports

3) EFFECT OF POLICIES ON TRANSPORTATION

ANOVA(b)

Model		Sum of Squares	df	Mean Square	F	Sig.
1	Regression	6.458	2	3.229	4.319	.020(a)
	Residual	29.161	39	.748		
	Total	35.619	41			

a Predictors: (Constant), clear objectives and long term environmental plans, Explicit defination of environmental policy
b Dependent Variable: selection of cleaner transportation methods

Coefficients(a)

Model		Unstandardized Coefficients		Standardized Coefficients	t	Sig.
		B	Std. Error	Beta		
1	(Constant)	3.549	.681		5.210	.000

A11

Explicit defination of environmental policy	-.354	.179	-.325	-1.980	.055
clear objectives and long term environmental plans	.389	.137	.466	2.845	.007

a Dependent Variable: selection of cleaner transportation methods

Printed in Great Britain
by Amazon

75346819R00137